HUGO'S
FRENCH
PHRASE BOOK

Published by

Hugo's Language Books Limited

104 JUDD STREET, LONDON, WC1H 9NF

FIRST PUBLISHED 1970

© 1970 Hugo's Language Institute Ltd.

ISBN: 085285 004 2

Latest reprint 1976

Facts and figures given in this book were correct when printed. If you discover any changes, please write to us.

Printed in Great Britain by
The Anchor Press Ltd, Tiptree, Essex

Contents

Introduction

This is primarily a phrase book in which selections of everyday words and phrases, complete with imitated pronunciation, are grouped under the usual headings of "Hotel", "Motoring", "Shopping" and so on. There are also conversion tables for weights, measures, distances, tyre pressures and clothing sizes.

In addition to the general notes that accompany each heading, there is more detailed information on French history, regions, social habits, traditional festivals, food and wine. It sometimes happens that the tourist, despite his excellent intentions, causes both himself and his host unnecessary embarrassment by committing some innocent breach of local custom or etiquette. We hope that this book will enable you to avoid making such mistakes, as well as helping you to make yourself understood.

THE IMITATED PRONUNCIATION

When reading the imitated pronunciation, the same value should be given to all syllables as there is practically no stress in French words. Pronounce each syllable as if it formed part of an English word and you will be understood sufficiently well. But the exact sound can be more nearly obtained by remembering the following points:

r   (roman) is not to be pronounced at all.

ng   (roman) is also silent. It merely indicates that the preceding vowel has a nasal sound.

r	pronounced more strongly than in English.
sh	is like the **s** in **"measure"**.
er	is like the **u** in **"fur"**.
er	represents the same sound, but longer, with the **r** sounded.
er	is like the **e** in **"her"**, but more closed.
ăh	is a little shorter than the a in **"far"**.
E, EE	represent the sound of the French **u** (like **i** in **"his"** or **e** in **"she"**, pronounced with rounded lips.

Instead of putting the definite or indefinite article before nouns in the vocabulary lists we have given the gender only. This will enable you to precede the noun with either "a" or "the", depending on the prevailing circumstances. The notes on page 16 will help you further.

A Brief Background to France

France covers an area of 213,000 square miles compared with the 94,000 square miles of the United Kingdom, and her population is slightly less. Being divided into 94 *départements* (akin to counties) for administrative purposes, the country is more easily definable in terms of the old provinces. Each province shows you a different face and it is for you to choose the one which you prefer.

The Ile de France is the oldest and has Paris at its centre; within the surrounding forests are many places that conjure up visions of old France. Versailles, home of the French kings, is only 12 miles from Paris; La Malmaison, where Napoleon and Josephine resided, is two miles closer; not much further away are the châteaux of Chantilly and St. Germain-en-Laye. The old royal hunting forest of Fontainebleau and the medieval wonder of Chartres cathedral are both within easy reach of the capital.

The northern province of Normandy, with its coastal chain of holiday resorts – fashionable Deauville, Mont St. Michel – and the now historic invasion beaches, adjoins the north-western province of Brittany. Many a Breton will claim that Mont St. Michel belongs to Brittany; at one time the argument was resolved by whichever side of the Mont the river Couesnon ran at low tide, but now there is an artificial channel to the west, putting the Mont in Normandy.

Brittany has much in common with Cornwall, and there are any number of splendid resorts, picturesque fishing hamlets and excellent bathing beaches along the otherwise rocky coast.

To the east of Paris is the champagne-producing area around Reims and Châlons-sur-Marne, and to the south and west is the Loire valley that combines vineyards with those wonderful châteaux for which it is justly famous. Further south-west are the vineyards around Bordeaux; this is probably the most renowned wine-growing country in the world, producing such names as Graves and Sauternes.

East of Bordeaux, in the middle of France, is the Massif Central with its wild mountains, while to the south are the Pyrenees and the Basque country (which has an atmosphere all of its own). Follow the Pyrenees to the Mediterranean and you come to the sun-drenched Midi, where you can visit the much older Arc de Triomphe at Orange, the immortal bridge at Avignon, and the Roman city of Arles set in an area made ever-memorable by the paintings of Van Gogh.

The Riviera, or Côte d'Azur, is not far distant; this must surely be the most well known stretch of coastline in the world. Between the Riviera and Lake Geneva are the magnificent French Alps that culminate in Mont Blanc, the highest peak in Europe if one discounts the Russian Caucasus.

Whatever the tourist is seeking, he will find it in the varied land of France, backed up by a complete range of

8

hotels with every conceivable facility, and a cuisine which is unequalled throughout the world.

History. Between the time of the Roman retreat from Gaul and the mid-eleventh century, the most eminent figure of French history was Charlemagne, under whose dynasty the country was strong and independent. By the time William the Conqueror's descendants had claimed much of western France the country was in need of reunification. This was brought about by King Philip Augustus and Louis IX, and it resulted in a fruitful period of culture, power and stability. Then came the Hundred Years' War with England, which ended after Joan of Arc had re-awakened French patriotism. A further period of squabbles and fluctuating fortunes led to the Bourbon successes of the seventeenth century (Richelieu, Louis XIV). The excesses of Louis XV and Louis XVI led to the Revolution of 1789, when the Bastille was stormed on July 14th. Equal rights for all men being proclaimed, the people were still not satisfied, and in 1792 the king was overthrown and the First Republic set up. Robespierre's brief reign of terror came and went, and Napoleon Bonaparte began his rise to power, crowning himself emperor in 1804. He was finally defeated at Waterloo in 1815 and died in exile on St. Helena. After another attempt to tolerate Bourbon royalty, the revolutionaries proclaimed the Second Republic, under Napoleon's nephew, who waited four years and then called himself Napoleon III. He fell from power after the Franco-Prussian war in 1871 and the Third Republic came into being. This lasted until 1946, and the Fourth Republic, torn by rival left- and right-wing factions, gave way to the Fifth under the presidency of General de Gaulle in 1958.

Facts and Figures. France is the largest general producer of farm products in Western Europe. Her vineyards supply for world consumption over 1,650 million gallons of wine in 100 major varieties, with over 500 subsidiary variations. She also produces about 350 named cheeses.

Third to the U.S.A. and the U.S.S.R. in the production of iron ore, France ranks sixth in steel production and fourth in the automobile field. She has both the fastest railway locomotive in the world and highest *téléférique* railway – the Aiguille du Midi at 12,467 feet.

Her sons – and daughters – have been great inventors. Pasteur discovered the rabies vaccine; Marie Curie discovered radium. The cinematograph was invented by Louis Lumière, and all blind people thank Braille for his system of writing. In many other fields of discovery a Frenchman has been responsible for the initial idea that led to the actual invention.

Traditional Festivals

France's great day is the 14th July when they celebrate the storming of the Bastille in 1789. On this great national holiday the whole nation goes gay with dancing in the streets, military parades, fun and games for every one, and magnificent firework displays.

The Nice Carnival lasts for the entire month of February and features processions, the Battle of Flowers, and all manner of fêtes which draw people from all over France. Cannes always seems to have a festival in progress and most notable is the International Film Festival when international film stars, producers, directors and journalists gather in the town. Many provincial towns and cities hold festivals of music and drama. The musical festival at Aix-en-Provence is outstanding and another notable event is the drama festival at Avignon when the Théâtre National Populaire performs in a splendid setting. Regional fêtes and festivals are numerous and among these most picturesque occasions is the celebration of the Burgundy grape harvest, and the singing and dancing festivals in Auvergne, Alsace, the Basque Country and Provence.

Son et Lumière (Sound and Light) originated in France, at Chambord in 1952. This first attempt was an outstanding success and the idea quickly spread throughout France and to other countries – with different measures of success, for there is a wide difference between the average performer and the virtuoso.

In France these performances are a work of art and the listener is overcome with the fairytale magic of the night, as music, light and poetry unfold an unforgettable vision of French art and history. They begin at the châteaux of the Loire region at Easter and end about October 1st, with spectacular performances at Mont St. Michel, Versailles and Carcassonne.

A special brochure giving the dates and hours for visits, and suggested itineraries is available from: U.F.E.S.S.I., 127, avenue des Champs-Elysées, Paris, or from any local "syndicats d'initiative".

Breton "Pardons" are one of the most attractive features of Brittany. These religious festivals are held on dates fixed in advance when often hundreds and sometimes thousands of pilgrims in their traditional clothes collect together around a chapel. Each town, village and hamlet holds its own "pardon".

From March to July some of the world's greatest theatrical companies come to Paris to perform at the Théâtre de la Ville and the Théâtre National de l'Odéon, and there is a nightly change of programme in the State theatres; Comédie Française, Théâtre National Populaire, Théâtre de France, the Opéra and the Opéra Comique.

Social Habits and Customs

In no other European country is it more important to follow the accepted rules of social behaviour. In every social class French men and women firmly adhere to a fixed form of etiquette, and however innocently you may break the rules you will give offence. It is therefore an act of courtesy to remember the correct form in those situations that are almost certain to arise.

Never be too familiar. Whenever you are addressing anybody you should always use their title – Monsieur

Postage
will be
paid by
licensee

Do not affix Postage Stamps if posted in
Gt. Britain, Channel Islands or N. Ireland

BUSINESS REPLY SERVICE

Licence No. **WC 2852**

HUGO'S LANGUAGE BOOKS LTD

104 JUDD STREET

LONDON, WC1H 9NF

2

Hugo Cassette Courses

FRENCH - GERMAN
SPANISH - ITALIAN

Why is it that thousands upon thousands have chosen the Hugo method of learning languages? What is the secret underlying the world-wide popularity of this system?

It is because the Hugo Courses demand the minimum expenditure of time and effort in return for the maximum success - and because they have changed what was once a dull task into a very interesting subject.

Each Cassette Course consists of 4 cassette tape recordings and a textbook; grammar, conversation and general fluency are fully covered in this potent Audio-Visual combination of nearly five hours play-back and 200 pages of text.

Post this card for full details.

Name..

Address ....

....

(pronounced *mer-se-er*, Mr), Madame (*măh-dăhm*, Mrs) or Mademoiselle (*măhd-mo'ăh-zell*, Miss) – and make frequent use of the magic word "pardon" (*păhr-do*ng). When making any kind of request always add, or include in your context, "s'il vous plaît" (*sill voo play*, please). Although "merci" (*mair-se*) means "thank you", when accepting proffered assistance say "Oui, s'il vous plaît" as "merci" would paradoxically convey "No thank you".

You shake hands with men, women and children of all classes not only when introduced but at every meeting and departure, however frequent.

It is considered bad form to arrive on time to a social invitation. To arrive early is unforgivable. How late you may arrive depends on the nature of the function; from a few minutes for a simple meal to a couple of hours for a well-attended party.

Always discuss the food and be profuse with your thanks for the trouble taken by your hostess, otherwise she will think something does not meet with your approval. Take your drinks slowly and in moderation (remember that the French are far more used to a lot of wine with their meals than you probably are), and be lavish with your praises even though the brew may not suit your particular taste.

To avoid obvious embarrassment you should have a knowledge of the public notices since most of these directly affect you. Here are the more common ones:

Défense d'entrer No Entry
Défense de toucher Do not touch
Défense de fumer No smoking

13

Défense de cracher No spitting
Il est interdit de . . . It is forbidden to . . .
Vous êtes priés de . . . You are requested to . . .
Prenez garde au chien Beware of the dog
Peinture fraîche! Wet Paint
Tenir la gauche (droite) Keep to the left (right)
Propriété privée Trespassers will be prosecuted
Ouvert Open
Fermé Closed
Entrée Way in
Sortie Way out
Libre Vacant
Occupé Engaged

Useful Everyday Words and Phrases

about environ *ah*ng-*ve-ro*ng
above au-dessus *oh-de*r-sᴇ
across en travers *ah*ng *trăh-vair*
after après *ăh-pray*
again encore *ah*ng-*kor*
at à *ăh*
before avant *ăh-vah*ng
behind derrière *dayr-e-air*
beneath au-dessous *oh de*r-*soo*
between entre *ah*ng-*tr*
big grand *grah*ng
by auprès de *oh-pray de*r
cold froid *fro'ăh*

14

down en bas *ah*ng *bah*
drink (*v.*) boire *bo'ăh*r (*n.*) boisson *f.* bo'ăhss-ong
enough assez *ăhss-eh*
everybody tout le monde *too ler mong*d
everything tout *too*
everywhere partout *păhr-too*
far loin *lo-a*ng
fast vite *veet*
food nourriture *f. noo-re-tEEr*
good bon *bong*
here ici *e-se*
high haut *oh*
how comment *komm-ah*ng
in dans *dah*ng
inside à l'intérieur *ăh lang-teh-re-er*
left gauche *gohsh*
less moins *mwang*
like comme *komm*
little petit *per-te*
lost perdu *pair-d*E
many beaucoup *boh-koo*
mine à moi *ăh mwăh*
more plus *pl*E
near près *pray*
no non *nong*
open ouvert *oovair*
outside dehors *der-or*
right droite *dro'ăht*
somebody quelqu'un *kell-ku*ng
something quelque chose *kell-ker shohz*
there là *lăh*

15

this ceci *ser-se*
those ceux-là *ser-lah*
through par *păhr*
too aussi *ohss-e*
under sous *soo*
until jusqu'à *shEES-kăh*
up en-haut *ahng-oh*
very très *tray*
when quand *kahng*
where où *oo*
why pourquoi *poohr-kwăh*
without sans *sahng*
yes oui *oo-e*

"A", "an", or "one" is translated **un** (pronounced
ung) before masculine nouns, and **une** (EE*n*) before feminine nouns.

"The" is translated **le** (*ler*) before masculine singular
nouns, and **la** (*lăh*) before feminine singular nouns. Before
a vowel or silent h, use **l'** instead of **le** or **la**. Before plural
nouns of either gender, "the" is translated **les**. This is
pronounced *lay'z* if the noun begins with a vowel or silent
h, otherwise it is simply *lay*.

Could you direct me to . . . ?   Pourriez-vous   m'indiquer
                                    où se trouve . . . ?
        poor-re-eh-voo ma*ng-de-keh oo se*r *troov*
Do you speak English?   Parlez-vous anglais?
        păhr-leh voo ahng-glay
Go away!   Allez-vous-en!
        *ăh-leh-voo-z'ah*ng

16

Have you a list of excursions?   Avez-vous une liste d'excursions?
ăh-veh voo z'EEn list decks-kEEr-ss-e-ong

Have you anything cheaper?   Avez-vous quelque chose de moins cher?
ăh-veh voo kell-ker shohz der mwang shair

How are you?   Comment-allez-vous?
komm-ahng-t'ăh-leh-voo

How long does it take to ...?   Combien de temps faut-il pour ...?
kong-be-ang der tahng foh-till poohr

How much is it?   Combien coûte ceci?
kong-be-ang koot ser-se

I am English   Je suis anglais (anglaise)
sher swe z'ahng-glay (z'ahng-glayz)

I am very sorry   Excusez-moi
ecks-kE-zeh mwäh

I cannot speak French   Je ne parle pas français
sher ner păhrl păh frahng-say

I do not wish to speak to you   Je ne veux pas vous parler
sher ner ver păh voo păhr-leh

I do not understand   Je ne comprends pas
sher ner kong-prahng pah

I enjoyed myself immensely   Je me suis beaucoup amusé
sher mer swe boh-koo ăh-mE-zeh

I have lost my way   Je me suis perdu
sher mer swe pair-dE

I have no time   Je n'ai pas le temps
sher nay păh ler tahng

Is this enough?   Est-ce assez?
ayss ăhss-eh?

B   17

It is very good	C'est très bon
	say tray bong
Look!	Regardez*!*
	rer-găhr-deh!
Please write it down	Ecrivez-le s'il vous plaît
	eh-kre-veh ler sill voo play
Thank you for your hospitality	Je vous remercie de votre accueil
	sher voo rer-mair-se der votr ăh-ker-e
This is incorrect	Ceci est faux
	ser-se ay foh
We are in a hurry	Nous sommes pressés
	noo somm press-eh
What is that?	Qu'est-ce que c'est?
	kayss ker-say
What is the correct time?	Avez-vous l'heure exacte?
	ăh-veh voo ler egg-zăhckt
Where can I get a . . . ?	Où puis-je obtenir . . . ?
	oo pweesh ob-ter-neer
Would you please speak slowly?	Pourriez-vous parler lentement?
	poor-re-eh voo păhr-leh lahngt-mahng
Your good health	A votre santé
	ăh votr sahng-teh

DAYS OF THE WEEK, MONTHS AND SEASONS

Sunday dimanche *de-mahngsh*
Monday lundi *lung-de*
Tuesday mardi *măhr-de*

Wednesday mercredi *mair-krer-de*
Thursday jeudi *sher-de*
Friday vendredi *vahng-drer-de*
Saturday samedi *săhm-de*

January janvier *shahng-ve-eh*
February février *feh-vre-eh*
March mars *măhrss*
April avril *ăh-vreel*
May mai *may*
June juin *shwang*
July juillet *shwe-yay*
August août *oo*
September septembre *sayp-tahng-br*
October octobre *ock-tobr*
November novembre *nov-ahng-br*
December décembre *deh-sahng-br*

Spring le printemps *ler prang-tuhng*
Summer l'été *leh-teh*
Autumn l'automne *loh-tonn*
Winter l'hiver *le-vair*

NUMBERS

1	un, une *ung*, EE*n*	**5**	cinq *sangk*
2	deux *der*	**6**	six *siss*
3	trois *tro'ăh*	**7**	sept *sett*
4	quatre *kăh-tr*	**8**	huit *wit*

19

9 neuf *nerf*	**22** vingt-deux *vangt-der*
10 dix *diss*	**23** vingt-trois *vangt-tro'ăh*
11 onze *ongz*	**30** trente *trahngt*
12 douze *dooz*	**40** quarante *kăh-rahngt*
13 treize *trayz*	**50** cinquante *sang-kahngt*
14 quatorze *kăh-torz*	**60** soixante *so'ăhss-ahngt*
15 quinze *kangz*	**70** soixante-dix* *so'ăhss-ahngt-diss*
16 seize *sayz*	**80** quatre-vingts* *kăhtr-vang*
17 dix-sept *diss-sett*	**90** quatre-vingt-dix* *kăhtr-vang-diss*
18 dix-huit *deez-wit*	**100** cent *sahng*
19 dix-neuf *deez-nerf*	**200** deux cents *der-sahng*
20 vingt *vang*	**1000** mille *mill*
21 vingt et un *vang t'eh ung*	**2000** deux mille *der-mill*

* Note that **septante** (70), **octante** or **huitante** (80) and **nonante** (90) may be heard in parts of E. France as well as in French-speaking Belgium and Switzerland.

¼ un quart *ung kăhr*	¾ trois quarts *tro'ăh kăhr*

½ une moitié	⅓ un tiers
EEn *mwăh-te-eh*	ung *te-air*

1st le premier, la première *ler* pre*r*-me-eh, *lăh* pre*r*-me-air
2nd le (la) deuxième *ler* (*lăh*) der-ze-ame
3rd le (la) troisième *ler* (*lăh*) tro'ăh-ze-ame

TIME

today aujourd'hui *oh-shoohr-dwe*
yesterday hier e-*air*
tomorrow demain *der-ma*ng
last year l'année dernière *lăh-neh dair-ne-air*
next year l'année prochaine *lăh-neh prosh-ain*
this morning ce matin *ser măh-ta*ng
this afternoon cet après-midi *set'tăh-pray-me-de*
this evening ce soir *ser so'ăhr*
last night hier soir *e-air so'ăhr*
tomorrow night demain soir *der-ma*ng *so'ăhr*
next week la semaine prochaine *lăh ser-main prosh-ain*
last week la semaine dernière *lăh ser-main dair-ne-air*
minute minute *f. me-n*EEt
hour heure *f. er*
day jour *m. shoohr*
fortnight quinze jours *ka*ngz *shoohr*
month mois *m. mwăh*
early tôt *toh*
late tard *tăhr*
one o'clock une heure EEn *er*
13.00 hours treize heures *tray z'er*
quarter past one une heure et quart EEn *er eh kăhr*

21

13.15 hours* treize heures quinze *tray z'er kah*ngz
half past one une heure et demie EE*n er eh de*r *-me*
13.30 hours* treize heures trente *tray z'er trah*ngt
two o'clock deux heures *de*r *z'er*
three o'clock trois heures *tro'ăh z'er*
twelve o'clock douze heures *dooz er or* midi *me-de*
noon midi *me-de*
midnight minuit *me-nwe*

* The 24-hour clock is used in all timetables, and also verbally in enquiry offices, making business appointments and in most other 'official' situations.

COLOURS

black noir *no'ahr*
white blanc *blah*ng
red rouge *roosh*
orange orange *or-ah*ng-*sh*
yellow jaune *shohn*
green vert *vair*
blue bleu *bler*
indigo indigo *a*ng-*de-goh*
violet violet *ve-oll-ay*
brown marron *măh-ron*g
grey gris *gre*
beige beige *baish*
pink rose *rohz*
mauve mauve *mohv*
purple pourpre *poohr-pr*
dark foncé *fong-seh*
light clair *klair*

22

Hotels

France has some 14,000 hotels officially classified as Tourist Hotels by the Commissariat Général du Tourisme. These are identified by a red, white and blue sign which shows the exact category of the hotel. These categories are: four star – de luxe and first class hotels; three star – very comfortable hotels; two star—second class hotels; one star – third class hotels. Each of these categories is sub-divided into "A" "B" and "C", which, together with the four star "L" classification for de luxe hotels, gives the visitor a choice of 13 categories from which to choose.

In addition to the officially classified Tourist Hotels there are many others in which the rates, service and amenities differ considerably. Among these are:

Relais de Tourisme. Tourist hotels with a limited number of rooms but specializing in food of a very high standard.

Relais Routiers. Around 4,000 hotels and (mainly) restaurants, situated on main roads. The food is excellent, and the accommodation very reasonable; prices are surprisingly low.

Châteaux-Hôtels and Vieilles Demeures. The Association of French Châteaux-Hôtels has about 80 châteaux, manor houses and notable residences throughout the country which afford the tourist quiet, up-to-date comfort and first-rate food in beautiful and historical surroundings.

Relais de Campagne (The Country Inn organization) lists over 100 inns which are close to the main highways; most of them are in picturesque settings, and all provide excellent food.

Logis de France, Auberges de Vacances. This independent chain of hotels, situated off the beaten track, gives the motorist a rare opportunity to explore the deep countryside. A condition of the financial assistance they receive from the State is that they comply with a rigid set of standards as regards food, service and sanitation, and the rates are very reasonable. A complete list can be obtained from: Logis de France, 25 rue Jean Hermoz, Paris, 8, or from French Government Tourist Offices.

Motels

These are steadily increasing in number. They are already situated in: Aix-en-Provence, Les Angles (near Avignon), Antibes, Bédarrides (near Avignon), La Ciotat, Chonas (near Vienne), Les Houches, Mandelieu, Marseille, Pont-de-l'Isère, Roc-Amadour, Saint Aygulf, Saint-Jean-de-Luz, Les Saintes Maries-de-la-Mer, Le Touquet, Tresserve (near Aix-les-Bains), Ville-neuve-Loubet and Vouzon. Ask the French Government Tourist Office for an up-to-date list.

USEFUL WORDS AND PHRASES

basin lavabo *m. lăh-văh-bo*
bath baignoire *f. bain-yo'ăhr*
bathroom salle de bain *f. săhl der bang*

bed lit *m. lee*

bedroom chambre *f. shah*ng-*br*
    (single) — pour une personne *poohr* EEn *pair-sonn*
    (double) — pour deux personnes *poohr der pair-sonn*

bill (restaurant) addition *f. äh-de-se-*ong

bill (hotel) note *f. not*

blanket couverture *f. koo-vair-t*EEr

board (full) pension complète *f. pah*ng-*se-*ong *k*ong-*playt*

board (half) demi pension *f. der-me pah*ng-*se-*ong

chair chaise *f. shayz*

chambermaid femme de chambre *f. fähmm der shah*ng-*br*

coat-hanger cintre *m. sang*tr

dining room salle à manger *f. sähl äh mah*ng-*sheh*

eiderdown édredon *m. eh-drer-d*ong

hotel hôtel *m. oh-tell*

hot water bottle bouillotte *f. boo'e-yot*

key clef *f. kleh*

lavatory toilettes *f. pl. to'äh-lett*

lift ascenseur *m. ähss-sah*ng-*ser*

manager directeur *m. de-reck-ter*

mattress matelas *m. mäht-läh*

page boy groom *m. groom*

pillow oreiller *m. or-ay'e-yeh*

porter porteur *m. por-ter*

proprietor propriétaire *m. prop-re-eh-tair*

radiator radiateur *m. räh-de-äh-ter*

reading lamp lampe de chevet *f. lah*ngp *der sher-v*

sheet drap *m. dräh*

shutters volets *m. pl. voll-ay*

soap savon *m. säh-v*ong

switch interrupteur *m. ang-tair-*rEEp-*ter*

table table *f.* *tăh-bl*
tap (hot, cold) robinet *m.* (chaud, froid)
    rob-e-nay (*shoh, fro'ăh*)
towel serviette *f.* *sair-ve-ett*
wardrobe armoire *f.* *ăhr-mo'ăhr*
window fenêtre *f.* *fer-nay-tr*

I am Mr (Mrs) Je suis Monsieur (Madame)
    sher swee meɪ-se-eɪ (*măh-dăhm*)
Have you a room for one Avez-vous une chambre
night? pour une nuit?
    ăh-veh voo EEn *shahng-br poohr* EEn *nwee*
I (we) wish to stay . . . days – J'aimerais (nous aimerions)
1 week – 2 weeks rester . . . jours – une
    semaine – deux semaines
    shaym-ray (*nooz'ay-*meɪ-*re-ong) ress-teh . . . shoohr*
    – EEn seɪ-*main – deɪ* seɪ-*main*
May I see the room? Pourrais-je voir la chambre?
    poo-raysh vo'ăhr lăh shahng-br
I want a room for myself only Je veux une chambre pour
    moi seul
    sher veɪ EEn *shahng-br poohr mwah* serl
Have you a room with a Avez-vous une chambre
private bathroom? avec salle de bain?
    ăh-veh voo EEn *shchng-br ăh-veck săhl de*ɪ *bang*
Any room will do Je. prendrais n'importe
    quelle chambre
    *she*ɪ *prahng-dray na*ng-*port kell shahng-br*
It is too noisy C'est trop bruyant
    *say tro br*E-*yah*ng

Can I overlook the sea (the garden)?	Avez-vous une chambre donnant sur la mer (le jardin)?

ăh-veh voo EEn shang-br donn-ahng SEEr lăh mair (ler shăhr-dang)

Where is the bathroom?	Où est la salle de bain?

oo ay lăh săhl der bang

I only require breakfast	Je ne veux que le petit déjeuner

sher ner ver ker ler per-te deh-sher-neh

May I have breakfast in my room?	Pourrais-je avoir mon petit déjeuner dans ma chambre?

poo-raysh ăh-vo'ăhr mong per-te deh-sher-neh dahng măh shahng-br

I require breakfast and an evening meal	Je veux le petit déjeuner et le dîner

sher ver ler per-te deh-sher-neh eh ler de-neh

I require full board	Je veux la pension complète

sher ver lăh pahng-se-ong kong-playt

Does that include all services and taxes?	Est-ce que le service et les taxes sont compris?

ayss-ker ler sair-viss eh lay tăhx song kong-pre

What do I do about laundry?	Vous chargez-vous du linge?

voo shăhr-sheh voo dE langsh

May I have a pillow (a towel)?	Pourrais-je avoir un oreiller (une serviette)?

poo-raysh ăh-vo'ăhr ung or-ay'e-yeh – EEn sair-ve-ett

May I have an extra blanket?	Pourrais-je avoir une autre couverture?

poo-raysh ăh-vo'ăhr EEn oh-tr koo-vair-tEEr

27

Can I have a stronger light? Est-ce que je peux avoir une lumière plus forte?
*ayss-ke*r *she*r *pe*r *ăh-vo'ăh*r EEn lE-*me-air* plE *fort*

I am going to bed Je vais me coucher
*she*r *vay me*r *koo-sheh*

Please call me at . . . Pourriez-vous me réveiller à . . .?
*poo-re-yeh voo me*r *reh-vay'e-yeh ăh*

I shall be back at . . . Je serai de retour à . . .
*she*r *se*r-*ray de*r *re*r-*toohr ăh*

Please open (close) the window Pourriez-vous ouvrir (fermer) la fenêtre?
*poo-re-yeh voo oo-vree*r (*fair-meh*) *lăh fer-nay-t*r

I would like a hot bath J'aimerais prendre un bain chaud
*shaym-ray prah*ng*d*r *u*ng *ba*ng *shoh*

May I have some drinking water? Pourrais-je avoir une carafe d'eau?
*poo-raysh ăh-vo'ăh*r EEn *kăh-răhf doh*

I need these clothes washed J'aimerais faire laver ces affaires
shaym-ray fair lăh-veh say z'ăh-fair

Can I have them back tomorrow? Pourrais-je les avoir pour demain?
*poo-raysh lay z'ăh-vo'ăh*r *poohr de*r-*ma*ng

Would you repair this?	Pourriez-vous me faire réparer ceci?
	*poo-re-yeh voo me*r *fair reh-păh-reh se*r*-se*
Would you dry these shoes (clothes) for me?	Pourriez-vous me faire sécher ces chaussures (vêtements)?
	*poo-re-yay voo me*r *fair seh-sheh say shohss-*EE*r (vaytt-mah*ng)
What time do you close?	A quelle heure fermez-vous?
	*ăh kell e*r *fair-meh voo*
May I have that table?	Pourrais-je avoir cette table?
	poo-raysh ăh-vo'ăhr sett tăh-bl
May I dine now?	Pourrais-je dîner tout de suite?
	poo-raysh de noh toot sweet
May I dine earlier (later) tomorrow?	Pourrais-je dîner plus tôt (plus tard) demain?
	*poo-raysh de-neh pl*E *to (pl*E *tăhr) der-ma*ng
May I have my bill?	Voulez-vous me donner l'addition (la note*)?
	*voo-leh voo me*r *donn-eh lăh-de-se-o*ng *(lăh not)*
	* Use this when you mean the hotel bill
Where is my luggage?	Ou sont mes bagages?
	*oo so*ng *may băh-găhsh*
Would you get me a taxi?	Pourriez-vous m'appeler un taxi?
	*poo-re-yeh voo măhp-leh u*ng *tăhx-e*

Camping and Caravanning

There are more than 3,600 recognized camping grounds in France and also tent and hut villages for campers all along the Riviera and Basque coasts. Full information can be obtained from the Camping Club de France, 218 Boulevard Saint-Germain, Paris, 7, or the Fédération Française de Camping et de Caravanning, 78 rue de Rivoli, Paris, 4, who publish a Camping Guide and map, also available from French Government Tourist Offices.

Nearly all official camping sites have an enclosure under constant supervision, running water, washing places, wash houses, hygienic lavatories, a refuse-clearance service, and facilities for buying food etc. in or near the camp. The fees are established by Prefectural decrees and clearly displayed at all camp entrances.

Outside of officially laid out establishments, camping in France is free. It is however essential that the camper observes police and health rules. Permission to pitch a tent must also be sought from the owner of the land and before camping in the State-controlled forests (forêts domaniales) campers must produce for the forester the vignette of the Fédération Française de Camping et de Caravanning or the camping "carnet" of either the Fédération Internationale de Camping et de Caravanning or the Alliance Internationale de Tourisme. The forester will then direct the camper to an authorized site.

Youth Hostels. There are more than 300 Youth Hostels in France which are available to anybody who holds an international camping passport or a card issued by the French Youth Hostel Federation. Most French hostels provide only the bare essentials and for further detailed information you should consult your own Youth Hostel association or the Fédération Unie des Auberges de la Jeunesse, 11 bis, rue de Milan, Paris, 9, or the Ligue Française pour les Auberges de la Jeunesse, 38 Boulevard Raspail, Paris, 7.

USEFUL WORDS AND PHRASES

boots bottes *f. bott*
bridge pont *m. po*ng
bucket seau *m. soh*
camp (v.) camper *kah*ng*-peh*
camping site camping *m. kah*ng*-ping*
cooking utensils instruments de cuisine *m.*
        *a*ng*ss-*tre*-mah*ng *der* kwee-*zeen*
cork screw tire-bouchon *m. teer-boo-sho*ng
drinking water eau potable *f. oh pot-ăh-bl*
east est *m. esst*
farm ferme *f. fairm*
farmer fermier *m. fair-me-eh*
field champ *m. shah*ng
forest forêt *f. for-ay*
frying pan poêle *f. po'ăhl*
groundsheet tapis de sol *m. tăh-pe der sol*
hike (v.) faire du footing *fair d*e *foo-ting*
hitch hike (v.) faire de l'auto-stop *fair der loh-toh-stop*
hill côte *f. koht*
ice glace *f. glăhss*

31

lake lac *m. lăhck*
log bûche *f. bEEsh*
matches allumettes *f. ăh-lE-mett*
mess tin gamelle *f. găh-mell*
methylated spirit alcool à brûler *m. ăhl-ko-ol ăh brE-leh*
mountain montagne *f. mong-tăhn-yer*
mountain pass col *m. kol*
north nord *m. nor*
paraffin pétrole *m. peh-troll*
path chemin *m. sher-mang*
penknife canif *m. kăh-niff*
picnic pique-nique *m. peek-neek*
pole mât *m. mah*
river (small) rivière *f.,* (main) fleuve *m. re-ve-air, flery*
road route *f. root*
rope corde *f. kord*
rubbish ordures *f. or-dEEr*
refuse bin boîte à ordures *f. bo'ăht ah or-dEEr*
rucksack sac à dos *m. săhck ăh doh*
saucepan casserole *f. kăhss-rol*
shower douche *f. doosh*
sleeping bag sac de couchage *m. săhck der koo-shăhsh*
snow neige *f. naysh*
south sud *m. sEEd*
storm orage *m. or-ăhsh*
stove réchaud *m. reh-shoh*
stream cours d'eau *m. koohr doh*
summit sommet *m. somm-ay*
tent tente *f. tahngt*
tent peg piquet *m. pe-kay*
thermos thermos *f. tair-moss*

tin opener ouvre-boîtes *m.* *oovr-bo'äht*
torch lampe de poche *f.* *lah*ng*p der posh*
valley vallée *f.* *väh-leh*
village village *m.* *ve-lähsh*
walk (v.) se promener *ser promm-neh*
walk (n.) promenade *f.* *promm-nähd*
waterfall cascade *f.* *kähss-kähd*
waterproof imperméable *m.* *ang-pair-meh-äh-bl*
weather (bad, good) (mauvais, beau) temps *m.*
                        *(moh-vay, boh) tah*ng
west ouest *m.* *west*
wind vent *m.* *vah*ng
wood bois *m.* *bo'äh*
youth hostel auberge de jeunesse *f.* *oh-bairsh der sher-ness*

May I camp here?   Est-ce que je puis camper
                              ici?
        *ess ker sher pwee kah*ng*-peh e-se*
Where is the caravan site? Où est le terrain de camp-
                              ing?
        *oo ay ler tay-rah*ng *der kah*ng*-ping*
What is the charge per night? Combien est-ce par nuit?
        *kong-be-a*ng *ess pährr nwee*
May we light a fire?   Est-ce que l'on peut faire du
                              feu?
        *ess ker long per fairr d*E *fer*
Where can I buy . . . ?   Où puis-je acheter . . . ?
        oo pwee-sh ähsh-teh

C   33

Motoring

France has an average of two miles of road to every square mile, a figure not exceeded by any other country in the world. Every village, however remote, and every beauty spot is accessible to the motorist. The great trunk roads (Routes Nationales) permit high average speeds on long journeys, and for those who are in no hurry – or who want to avoid heavy traffic – there is an endless selection of good secondary roads. There should never be any fear of losing the way as the signposts are universally recognized as being as frequent and clear as possible. There are also several sections of motorway; on some you must pay a toll upon leaving (Autoroutes à péage) but others are free. The mountain roads of France are supreme engineering achievements and are so carefully graded that the steepest climb – or descent – need have no terrors for the driver.

To drive a car in France you need a driving licence and a log book. No Customs document is required if the motorist's stay is not to exceed six months. The vehicle must carry its national identification sign (black letters on white background). Outside built-up areas, crash helmets must be worn by all drivers and passengers on motorcycles, scooters and mo-peds.

Insurance. All types of motor car, motor cycle, coach, lorry, van, scooter and mo-ped must be insured in France and visitors are called upon to conform to this regulation. They must produce an International Insurance Certificate (Green Card) or an Insurance Certificate issued by a French Company, on arrival at the port, airport or land frontier post of entry. If neither of these can be produced drivers may enter the country if they take out frontier-issued insurance cover (Assurance Frontière) obtainable at the Customs Office. This is a short term policy valid only for France and is issued for a 2-day, 7-day or 21-day period. The period originally subscribed cannot be extended, so if the motorist wishes to prolong his stay he must take out a further policy with a French Company or have received a valid Green Card from his own country of residence.

In case of accident. If in a town get a police officer (Agent de Police) to make a report ("dresser un constat"). In the country, if any injury has been suffered, advise the Gendarmerie or ensure that somebody does so; get a report made by a Huissier (Sheriff's Officer) from the nearest town. It is always advisable to secure witnesses and whenever possible photographs should be taken.

Immediately advise the Bureau Central Français des Sociétés d'Assurances contre les Accidents d'Automobiles (Central Office for French Motor Accident Insurance Companies), 18 rue de Tocqueville, Paris 17e. Tel. 622-08-90 to 08-94.

Fuel and oil. All major brands of lubricating oils are on sale in France. Two grades of petrol are available, with a possible slight variation in prices from region to region; standard ("ordinaire") and premium ("super-carburant") which is better suited to high compression engines.

Repair and breakdown services. Under the auspices of the Touring Club de France, the Secours Routier Français has been formed; this includes a breakdown service. Special telephones indicated by road signs are spaced at every 2½ miles along the principal main roads. Help may be obtained day and night from the nearest Commissariat de Police or Gendarmerie, or from a competent repairer. A list of telephone sites and repair-points is included on all the route maps issued by the Touring Club de France, prepared in co-operation with the Alliance Internationale de Tourisme.

Principal rules of the road. Drivers must keep as close to the right-hand side of the road as conditions permit. Other vehicles are overtaken on the left.

A solid line in the centre of the road must never be crossed or overridden. A broken central line may be crossed for the purpose of overtaking another vehicle or crossing the road. Double lines, one continuous and the other broken, may be crossed only where the broken line is immediately to the driver's left. Double lines must not be crossed when the continuous line is nearest to the driver's left-hand side.

Sound your horn only in cases of real need. In Paris and some other cities, the use of the horn is forbidden except in cases or urgent danger. During the night, head-light signals replace sound signals.

To turn right at a crossing, signal and keep as close as possible to the nearside kerb, making a narrow turn. To turn left, go as close as possible to the middle of the road and turn near the centre of the junction, taking care not to enter the new road on the left-hand side. Such advice may seem elementary, but it is easy to forget where you are and to make your turns as if you were back in Britain.

A recently introduced rule is that seat belts must be worn outside towns.

Speed limits. In built up areas vehicles must not exceed 60 kilometres per hour (37 m.p.h.). Some urban areas have a lower speed limit than this, which is indicated at the point where it comes into force. Outside urban areas there is a speed limit of 100 km.p.h. (62 m.p.h.) on all roads except motorways or if otherwise specified.

Overtaking. With few exceptions, overtaking is done on the left. It may however be done on the right-hand side of a vehicle if the driver of the latter has signalled that he is going to turn left, after he has pulled out towards his left. Trams should be overtaken on the right, provided there is space to do so between them and the road edge. Do not overtake on hill tops or at turnings, or when visibility is limited, and do not place too much trust in your front seat passenger's assurances that it is safe to do so! Overtaking is forbidden at non-guarded level crossings and at cross-roads where no priorities exist. Three-lane roads are divided by broken lines. The extreme left-hand lane must never be used for overtaking.

Right of way. In built up areas, vehicles coming from the right have right of way.

Outside urban areas, drivers on principal through roads (routes à grande circulation) have the right of way.

Such roads are clearly marked on most maps. On other roads the right of way is indicated by road signs marked "passage protégé"; this shows that there are halt signs on the side roads.

Other than on priority roads as described above, when two vehicles meet at cross-roads, the one on the left of the other must give way.

Parking. It is forbidden to park where this interferes with the movement of other vehicles or pedestrians, or obstructs entrances to buildings. Even when there are no signs indicating "no parking", it is forbidden to park wherever visibility is insufficient, as at cross-roads, hill-tops and turnings.

The "No parking" sign is round, with a red edge and a red diagonal stripe against a blue ground. Where parking is allowed (usually on one side of the street only) this sign will have below it a small white rectangular notice stating the times and sides allowed. In general, such parking is allowed on the odd numbered side of the street from the 1st to the 15th of the month. From the 16th to the end of the month it is on the even side.

In Paris and some other cities there are "zones bleues", all clearly marked, where parking is permitted for one hour from 9 a.m. till 12.30 p.m. and from 2.30 p.m. till 7 p.m. except on Sundays and public holidays. In these zones, the use of a card showing time of arrival and latest time for departure is obligatory. These cards, "disques de stationement", must be displayed inside the windscreen and may be obtained free at the Préfecture de Police, at Commissariats de Police or from Motor Clubs, etc.

In Paris and the immediate surroundings (département de la Seine) where there are no other indications, drivers must park on the right-hand side of the road in the direction the car is travelling. Only in one-way streets is left-hand side parking permitted.

Lighting. It is an offence to dazzle other drivers.

Amber headlights are obligatory for French drivers and it is strongly recommended that those coming from other countries where white headlights are still used should conform to the French custom. Amber bulbs, headlight discs and easily removed varnish for headlight glasses provide suitable solutions.

Between sunset and dawn and at other times of bad visibility, particularly during fog, stationary vehicles must show a clearly visible light in front and at the rear. Such lights must be on that side of the vehicle which is nearest to the centre of the road.

This rule does not apply to Paris and its immediate surroundings (département de la Seine) provided that the vehicle is clearly visible by other means such as street lighting for a distance of 100 metres. Similar exceptions apply to some other localities.

USEFUL WORDS AND PHRASES

accelerator accélérateur *m. ahck-seh-leh-răh-ter*
back axle pont arrière *m. pong ăh-re-air*
battery batterie *f. băht-ree*
big end tête de bielle *f. tayt der be-ell*
body châssis *m. shahss-e*

bolt boulon *m. boo-lo*ng
bonnet capot *m. kăh-poh*
boot coffre *m. kofr*
brake frein *m. fra*ng
    (handbrake) frein à main *m. fra*ng *ăh mah*ng
brake lining garniture de frein *f. găhr-ne-t*EE*r de*r *fra*ng
breakdown panne *f. păhn*
breakdown van voiture de dépannage *f.*
        *vo'äht*EE*r de*r *deh-pah-nash*
bumper pare-chocs *m. păhr-shock*
camshaft arbre à cames *m. ăhr-br ăh kăhm*
can bidon *m. be-do*ng
car voiture *f. vo'äh-t*EE*r*
caravan caravane *f. kăh-răh-văhn*
carburettor carburateur *m. kăhr-b*EE*-răh-ter*
choke starter *m. star-ter*
clutch embrayage *m. ah*ng*-bray-yăhsh*
distributor distributeur *m. diss-tre-b*E*-ter*
door portière *f. por-te-air*
drive (v.) conduire *ko*ng*-dwee*r
driver chauffeur *m. shoh-fer*
dynamo dynamo *f. de-năh-moh*
engine moteur *m. mot-er*
exhaust échappement *m. eh-shahp-mah*ng
fan ventilateur *m. vah*ng*-te-lăh-ter*
fan belt courroie de ventilateur *f. koo-ro'ăh de*r
        *vah*ng*-te-lăh-ter*
funnel entonnoir *m. ah*ng*-tonn-o'ăhr*
garage garage *m. găh-rahsh*
gear vitesse *f. ve-tess*
gear-box boîte de vitesses *f. bo'äht de*r *ve-tess*

gear lever levier de vitesses *m. ler-ve-eh-der ve-tess*
handle manivelle *f. măh-ne-vell*
hood capote *f. kăh-pot*
horn klaxon *m. klăhck-song*
highway code code de la route *m. kod der lăh root*
hub moyeu *m. mo'ăh-yer*
ignition allumage *m. ăh-lE-mahsh*
ignition key clef de contact *f. kleh der kong-tahckt*
indicator clignotant *m. kleen-yot-ahng*
inner tube chambre à air *f. shahng-br ăh air*
jack cric *m. kre*
licence permis *m. pair-mee*
lights (head) phares *m. făhr*
lights (side) feux de position *m. fer der poh-ze-se-ong*
lights (rear) feux arrière *m. fer ăh-re-air*
lorry camion *m. kăh-me-ong*
lubrication graissage *m. grayss-ăhsh*
mechanic mécanicien *m. meh-kăh-ne-se-ung*
mirror rétroviseur *m. reh-tro-ve-zer*
motorway autoroute *f. oh-toh-root*
number plate plaque d'immatriculation *f.*
　　　　　　　plăhck de-măh-tre-kEE-lăh-se-ong
nut écrou *m. eh-kroo*
oil huile *f. weel*
pedestrian piéton *m. pe-eh-tong*
petrol essence *f. he-sahngss*
petrol pump pompe à essence *f. pongp ah eh-sahngss*
piston ring segment de piston *m sehg-măhng der piss-tong*
plug bougie *f. boo-shee*
propeller shaft arbre de transmission *m.*
　　　　　　　ahrbr der trahngss-me-se-ong

radiator radiateur *m. răh-de-ăh-ter*
rim jante *f. shah*ngt
screw vis *f. veess*
screwdriver tournevis *m. toohr-ner-viss*
shock absorber amortisseur *m. ăh-mor-tiss-er*
skid déraper *deh-răh-peh*
spanner clé *f. kleh*
spares pièces de rechange *f. pe-ess der rer-shah*ng*sh*
speed vitesse *f. ve-tess*
speed limit limite de vitesse *f. lee-meet der ve-tess*
speedometer indicateur de vitesse *m.*
　　　　　　*a*ng*-de-kăh-ter der ve-tess*
spring ressort *m. rer-sor*
starter démarreur *m. deh-măh-rer*
steering wheel volant *m. voll-ah*ng
tank réservoir à essence *m. reh-zair-vo'ăhr ăh eh-sah*ngss
traffic lights feux *m. fer*
trailer remorque *f. rer-mork*
transmission transmission *f. trah*ngss*-me-se-o*ng
two-stroke mixture mélange deux temps *m.*
　　　　　　*meh-lah*ng*sh der tah*ng
tyre pneu *m. pner*
tyre (tubeless) pneu à chambre incorporée *m.*
　　　　　　*pner ah shang-br a*ng*-kor-poh-reh*
valve valve *f. văhlv*
vehicle véhicule *f. veh-e-kEEl*
washer rondelle *f. rong-dell*
wheel roue *f. roo*
　　(rear wheel) roue arrière *roo ăh-re-air*
　　(front wheel) roue avant *roo ăh-vah*ng
　　(spare wheel) roue de secours *roo der ser-koohr*

window glace *f. glăhss*
    (rear window) glace arrière *glăhss ah-re-air*
windscreen pare-brise *m. pahr-breez*
windscreen wiper essuie-glace *m. eh-swee-glăhss*
wing aile *f. ayl*

I want some petrol   J'aimerais de l'essence (de
(oil, water)   l'huile, de l'eau)
   shaym-ray der leh-sahngss (der lweel, de loh)

Would you check the oil?   Voulez-vous vérifier le
                        niveau de l'huile?
   voo-leh voo veh-re-fe-eh ler ne-voh der lweel

Would you check the tyre   Voulez-vous vérifier la
pressure?   pression des pneus?
   voo-leh voo veh-re-fe-eh lăh press-e-ong day pner

My car has broken down   Ma voiture est en panne
— km. from here   à — km. d'ici
măh vo'ăh-tEEr ay tahng păhnn ăh—ke-loh-met-tr de-se

Do you do repairs?   Faites-vous des répara-
                        tions?
   fayt voo day reh-păh-răh-se-ong

Can you repair the ... ?   Pouvez vous reparer le
                        (la) ... ?
   poo-veh voo reh-păh-reh ler (lăh)

How long will it take?	Combien de temps cela prendra-t-il?

kong-be-ang der tahng ser-lăh prahng-drăh till

I have run out of petrol	Je n'ai plus d'essence

sher nay plE deh-sahngss

The engine is overheating	Le moteur chauffe

ler mo-ter shohf

May I park here?	Est-ce que je peux stationner ici?

ess-ker sher per stăh-se-onn-eh e-se

Where may I park?	Où est-ce que je peux stationner?

oo ess-ker sher per stăh-se-onn-eh

How far is it to ... ?	A quelle distance se trouve ... ?

ăh kell diss-tahngss ser troov

What time does the garage close?	A quelle heure ferme le garage?

ăh kell er fairm ler găh-rahsh

My brakes are slipping (binding)	Mes freins patinent (se bloquent)

may frang păh-teen (ser block)

How far is the next garage?	A quelle distance se trouve le prochain garage?

ăh kell diss-tahngss ser troov ler prosh-ang găh-rahsh

May I wash my hands?	Est-ce que je peux me laver les mains?
	ess-ker sher per mer lăh-veh lay mang
Where is the toilet, please?	Où sont les toilettes s'il vous plaît?
	oo song lay to'ah-lett sill voo play
May I use your telephone?	Est-ce que je peux me servir de votre téléphone?
	ess-ker sher per mer sair-veer der votr teh-leh-fon
I want a new fanbelt	Je veux une nouvelle courroie de ventilateur
	sher ver EEn noo-vell koo-ro'ăh der vahng-te-lăh-ter
The clutch is slipping	L'embrayage patine
	lahng-bray-yăhsh păh-teen
Is this the road to . . . ?	Est-ce la route pour . . . ?
	ess lăh root poohr
Would you wipe the windscreen?	Voulez-vous m'essuyer le parebrise?
	voo-leh voo meh-swee-yeh ler pahr-breez
Could you clean it right away?	Este-ce que vous pourriez le laver tout de suite?
	ess-ker voo poo-re-yeh ler lăh-veh toot-sweet
May I park without lights?	Est-ce que je peux stationner sans feux?
	ess-ker sher per stăh-se-onn-eh sahng fer
I want to hire a car for . . .	Je veux louer une voiture pour . . .
	sher ver loo-eh EEn vo'ăh-tEEr poohr

Would you fit a new bulb?	Voulez-vous poser une nou-velle lampe?
voo-leh voo poh-zeh EEn *noo-vell lah*ngp	
Would you mend this puncture?	Voulez-vous réparer cette crevaison?
voo-leh voo reh-pāh-reh sett *kre*r-*vay-zo*ng	
May I borrow ... ?	Est-ce que je peux em-prunter ...?
*ess-ke*r *she*r *pe*r *ah*ng-*pru*ng-*teh* ...	

Public Transport

BY RAIL

French Railways (S.N.C.F.) provide about 25,000 miles of track served by some 5,000 stations. French trains are both fast (they average 68 m.p.h.) and punctual and have two classes, first and second. The long-distance trains invariably include a dining car and on overnight trips there is a choice of first or second class couchettes (a mixed compartment), or the slightly more expensive but more comfortable first or second class Wagon-Lit sleeper.

Fare Reductions. Group travel and tourist tickets are subject to price reductions. Children up to four years of age travel free, and at half-fare between four and ten years. Full details of reductions and fares can be obtained from French Railways or a Travel Agent, who will also issue tickets and book seats.

Car-Sleeper Expresses. For motorists who don't like covering long distances French Railways run car-sleeper expresses. The car travels with the motorist whilst he sleeps to arrive fresh at his destination with hundreds of miles of road behind him.

The most popular routes with motorists from the United Kingdom are: Boulogne–Lyon, and during the summer months; Paris–Biarritz, Toulouse, Narbonne and Avignon. A service also operates between Le Touquet–Avignon and Narbonne.

USEFUL WORDS AND PHRASES

alight descendre *deh-sah*ng-*dr*
booking office guichet *m. ghe-shay*
carriage wagon *m, văh-gong*
case valise *f. văh-leez*
compartment compartiment *m. kong-păhr-te-mah*ng
corridor couloir *m. koo-lo'ahr*
dining car wagon-restaurant *m. văh-gong ress-tah-rah*ng
enquiry office bureau de renseignements *m.*
            *b*ɛ-*roh d*ɛ*r rah*ng-*sain-y*ɛ*r-mah*ng
entrance entrée *f. ah*ng-*treh*
exit sortie *f. sor-tee*
guard chef de train *m. sheff d*ɛ*r tra*ng
luggage van fourgon *m. foohr-gong*
luggage rack porte-bagages *m. port băh-găhsh*
platform quai *m. kay*
seat place *f. plăhss*
seat reservation réservation *f. reh-zair-văh-se-o*ng

47

*sleeper place de wagon-lit *f.* *plăhss* de**r** *văh-gong lee*
*sleeping berth couchette *f.* *koo-shett*
station gare *f.* *găhr*
station master chef de gare *m.* *sheff de*r *găhr*
ticket (single) billet (simple) *m.* *bee-yay* (*sang-pl*)
    (return) (billet) aller et retour
             (*bee-yay*) *ah-leh eh re*r-*toohr*
ticket collector contrôleur *m.* *kong-troh-le*r
timetable horaire *m.* *oh-rair*
train train *m.* *trang*
waiting room salle d'attente *f.* *săhl dăh-tah*ngt
window fenêtre *f.* *fe*r-*nay-tr*

* Remember that in a couchette compartment you must be prepared to share with five others, of either sex, while a sleeper is as on British trains.

I have a reserved seat	J'ai une place réservée
	sheh EEn *plăhss reh-zair-veh*
Would you find me a seat?	Pourriez-vous me trouver une place?
	*poo-re-yeh voo me*r *troo-veh* EEn *plăhss*
I would like a smoking (non smoking) compartment	J'aimerais un compartiment pour fumeurs (non fumeurs)
	*shaym-ray u*ng *kong-păhr-te-mah*ng *poohr fE-me*r (*nong fE-me*r)

Could I have a window seat?   Est-ce que je peux avoir une place à côté de la fenêtre?
ess ker sher per ăh-vo'ăhr EEn plähss ah koht-eh der lăh fer-nay-tr

This seat is reserved   Cette place est réservée
sett plähss ay reh-zair-veh

That seat is taken   Cette place est prise
sett plähss ay preez

Could you find me a berth?   Pourriez-vous me trouver une couchette?
poo-re-yeh voo mer troo-veh EEn koo-shett

May I open (close) the window?   Est-ce que je peux ouvrir (fermer) la fenêtre?
ess ker sher per oo-vreer (fair-meh) lăh fer-nay-tr

How long do we stop here?   Combien de temps s'arrête-t on ici?
kong-be-ang der tahng săhr-rayt-tong e-se

Where is the inspector?   Où est le contrôleur?
oo ay ler kong-troh-ler

Please mind my seat   Pourriez-vous me garder ma place?
poo-re-yeh voo mer găhr-deh măh plähss

Which way is the dining car?   De quel côté se trouve le wagon restaurant?
der kell koht-eh ser troov ler văh-gong ress-toh-rahng

What time is lunch (dinner)?   A quelle heure est le déjeuner (dîner)?
ah kell er ay ler deh-sher-neh (de-neh)

49

D

Porter, can you take this luggage to the left-luggage office?
Porteur, pourriez-vous me porter ces bagages à la consigne?
por-ter, poo-re-yeh voo mer por-teh say băh-găhsh ăh läh kong-seen-yer

I shall collect it at/on...
Je viendrai le chercher...
sher vee-ang-dray ler shair-sheh

Would you get me a taxi to...
Pourriez-vous m'appeler un taxi pour aller...
poo-re-yeh voo măhp-leh ung tăhx-e poohr ăh-leh...

Where is the booking office?
Où est le guichet?
oo ay ler ghe-shay

Where is the enquiry office?
Où est le bureau de renseignements?
oo ay ler be-roh der rahng-sain-yer-mahng

What time does the train leave for...?
A quelle heure part le train pour...?
ăh kell er păhr ler trang poohr

Which platform, please?
Quel quai, s'il vous plaît?
kell kay sill voo play

Is this the right train for...?
Est-ce bien le train pour...?
ess be-ang ler trang poohr

Does it go direct?
Est-ce qu'il est direct?
ess kill ay de-reckt

Must I change?
Est-ce que je dois changer?
ess ker sher do'ăh shahng-sheh

Where do I change?	Où est-ce que je dois chan-ger?
	oo ess ker sher do'ăh shang-sheh
What time is the last train for . . . ?	A quelle heure part le dernier train pour . . . ?
	ăh kell er păhr ler dair-ne-eh tra**ng** *poohr*
Where is the nearest hotel?	Où est l'hôtel le plus proche?
	*oo ay loh-tell ler pl***E** *prosh*

BY COACH, LOCAL TRANSPORT

The mainline railway stations are linked by bus with most French villages which do not have a railway station. Most of these connecting bus services are run in conjunction with French Railways and details can be obtained from French Railway Offices and stations, Information regarding the services operated by private firms can be obtained from the Fédération Nationale des Transports Routiers, 44, rue de la Bienfaisance, Paris. Tel. 522 71–30.

Although there are long-distance coach services, such as between Paris and the Riviera, and a considerable number of sight-seeing coach tours there is no coach service competitive with the railways such as exists in the United Kingdom.

There are regular bus or trolleybus services in all the main provincial towns and taxis operate in every town and city. However, it is in Paris that the majority of tourists will feel the need to use public transport, and the following information applies to systems run in the capital.

The Métro, the underground railway system, has virtually been designed for visitors. It is a one-price service regardless of distance; there are two classes and trains run from 5.30 a.m. to 12.30 a.m. approximately. It is cheap and economical and the method of indicating terminal directions, and the strategically placed maps, makes travel easy for the non-French speaking tourist.

The bus with the open rear platform which is so suitable for sightseeing is slowly disappearing. The passenger buys one ticket for each fare stage travelled (roughly at intervals of one mile). It is more economical to buy these tickets in booklet form ("carnets") and ask how many are needed for your destination. Most buses run between 7.30 a.m. and 9.30 p.m. but some lines operate until 12.30 a.m. On this late evening service ("service du soir") there is an additional charge of one ticket per journey. There is also a limited "service de nuit" which runs between the centre of Paris and the city boundaries. It leaves the Châtelet every hour between 1.30 a.m. and 5.30 a.m. and returns from the boundaries every hour between 1 am. and 5 a.m.

In addition to the saving made by buying books, there is a special tourist ticket, available for seven consecutive days, which entitles the visitor to unlimited first class travel by Métro or by bus. These tickets are available, on presentation of your passport, outside France at French Railways offices, at some travel agencies and banks, and in Paris from R.A.T.P. 53, Quai des Grands-Augustins, or Place de la Madeleine, or at the Welcome Bureau of the Comité de Tourisme de Paris, 7, rue Balzac.

Taxis are plentiful and cab ranks are nearly everywhere. Radio-taxis operate at any time of the day or night and will be sent immediately to any address.

Sight-seeing tours. If you are spending only a short time in Paris it is advisable to make sight-seeing tours by motor coach. One-day and half-day tours cover modern Paris, old Paris, an afternoon at Versailles, Fontainebleau, Chantilly or Chartres, Paris by night, floodlit Paris, and many of the most charming areas of the surrounding countryside. Travel agents, or your hotel, will give you full information and make your reservation. The famous "Bateaux-Mouche" boat trips on the Seine, through the heart of Paris, are another most popular and enjoyable way of seeing something of the lovely and historic capital.

USEFUL WORDS AND PHRASES

airport aéroport *m.* *ăh-eh-ro-por*
alight descendre *deh-sah*ng*-dr*
board monter *m*o*ng-teh*
boot coffre *m.* *kofr*
bus autobus *m.* *oh-toh-b*EES
case valise *f.* *văh-leez*
coach car *m.* *kăh*r
conductor contrôleur *m.* *k*o*ng-troh-ler*
connection correspondance *f.* *kor-ress-p*o*ng-dah*ngss
draught courant d'air *m.* *koo-rah*ng *dair*
driver chauffeur *m.* *shoh-fer*

fare tarif *m.* *tăh-riff*
front avant *ăh-vah*ng
fumes gaz *m.* *gahz*
rack porte-bagages *m.* *port băh-gahsh*
railway station gare *f.* *găhr*
rear derrière *dayr-e-air*
roof toit *m.* *to'ăh*
stop arrêt *m.* *ăh-ray*
terminus terminus *m.* *tair-me-nEES*
ticket (single) billet (simple) *m.* *bee-yay* (*sa*ng-*pl*)
   (return) (billet) aller et retour
          (*bee-yay*) *ăh-leh eh re*r*-toohr*
timetable horaire *m.* *oh-rair*
window fenêtre *f.* *fe*r*-nay-t*r

Where is the coach station? Ou est le terminus des cars
                    s'il vous plaît?
    *oo ay le*r *tair-me-nEE*s *day kăhr sill voo play*

I want a single (return) Je veux un billet simple
ticket to ... (d'aller et retour) pour ...
  *she*r *ve*r *u*ng *bee-yay sa*ng-*pl* (*dăh-leh eh re*r*-toohr*) *poohr* ...

What time do you leave A quelle heure partez-vous
(arrive)? (arrivez-vous)?
    *ăh kell e*r *păhr-teh voo* (*ăh-re-veh voo*)

I want to get off at ... Je veux descendre à ...
    *she*r *ve*r *deh-sah*ng-*d*r *ăh* ...

Will you tell me when we Pourriez-vous me prévenir
arrive? lorsque nous arriverons?
*poo-re-yeh voo me*r *prehv-neer lors-ke*r *noo z'ăh-re-ve*r*-ro*ng

Do you pass ... ?	Passez-vous par ... ?
	păhss-eh voo păhr ...
Do you go near ...?	Passez-vous près de ...?
	*păhss-eh voo pray de*r ...

Will you put this in the boot Pourriez-vous mettre ceci
(on the roof)? dans le coffre (sur le toit)?
*poo-re-yeh voo met-tr se*r-se dah*ng le*r kofr (SEE*r le*r to'*ăh*)

There is a draught Il y a un courant d'air
*ill e ăh u*ng koo-rah*ng dair*

Would you please open Pourriez-vous ouvrir (fer-
(close) the window? mer) la fenêtre?
*poo-re-yeh voo oo-vreer (fair-meh) lăh fe*r-*nay-tr*

May I put this on the rack? Est-ce que je peux mettre
ceci dans le porte-bagages?
*ess ke*r she*r pe*r *met-tr se*r-se dah*ng le*r port-băh-găhsh*

Do you return (start from) Est-ce que vous repartez
here? (partez) d'ici?
*ess ke*r voo re*r-păhr-teh (păhr-teh) de-se*

BY AIR

Air France operates a direct service between the United Kingdom and most of the principal cities in France, and internal connections are provided by Air-Inter.

The international airports for Paris are Orly and Le Bourget. Both are connected to the Invalides air terminal in Paris by means of a regular bus service. The magnificent international airport just outside Nice services the French Riviera.

French airport departure charges must be paid either when the ticket is bought, or at the airport.

USEFUL WORDS AND PHRASES

air hostess hôtesse (de l'air) *f. oh-tess* (der *lair*)
airline ligne aérienne *f. leen-yer ăh-eh-re-ayn*
airport aéroport *m. ăh-eh-ro-por*
case valise *f. văh-leez*
cloudy nuageux *nE-ah-sher*
control tower tour de contrôle *f. toohr* der *kong-trohl*
crew équipage *m. eh-ke-păhsh*
fog brouillard *m. broo'e-yăhr*
jet aircraft avion à réaction *m.*
        ăh-ve-ong ăh reh-ăhck-se-ong
land (v.) atterrir *ăh-tay-reer*
pilot pilote *m. pe-lot*
propeller hélice *f. eh-liss*
rack porte-bagages *m. port-băh-găhsh*
route route *f. root*
runway piste *f. pisst*
seat place *f. plăhss*
seat belt ceinture de sécurité *f.*
        *sang-*TEE*r* der *seh-*kE*-re-teh*
steward steward *m. s*tE*-wahrd*
take-off décollage *m. deh-koh-lahsh*
window fenêtre *f. fer-nay-tr*
wing aile *f. ayl*

When can I get a plane for . . . ?	Quand y a-t-il un avion pour . . . ?
*kah*ng *e ah-till u*ng *ăh-ve-o*ng *poohr . . .*	
What time does it leave (arrive)?	A quelle heure décolle t-il (arrive t-il)?
ăh kell er deh-koll till (ah-reev till)	
Where does it touch down?	Où est-ce qu'il atterrit?
oo ess kill ăh-tay-re	
Will you fasten (unfasten) my safety belt?	Pourriez-vous m'attacher (me défaire) ma ceinture de sécurité?
*poo-re-yeh voo măh-tăh-sheh (mer deh-fair) măh sa*ng-*tEEr der seh-kE-re-teh*	
Have you a map of the route?	Avez-vous une carte du trajet?
ăh-veh voo zEEn kăhrt dE trăh-shay	
Will you adjust my seat?	Pourriez-vous me régler mon fauteuil?
*poo-re-yeh voo mer reh-gleh mo*ng *foh-ter'e*	
What is the weather report?	Quelles sont les prévisions météorologiques?
*kell so*ng *lay preh-ve-se-o*ng *meh-teh-oroh-losh-ick*	
May I have some cigarettes (brandy)?	Est-ce que je peux avoir des cigarettes (du cognac)?
ess ker sher per ăh-vo'ahr day se-găh-rett (dE kon-yăhck)	
Are we on time?	Sommes-nous à l'heure?
somm noo zăh ler	

Would you adjust the air conditioner?	Pourriez-vous me régler le climatiseur?
	poo-re-yeh voo mer reh-gleh ler kle-mah-te-zer
It is very warm	Il fait très chaud
	ill fay tray shoh
I do not feel well	Je ne me sens pas bien
	sher ner mer sahng păh be-ang

Food and Wine

It is difficult to write briefly of the pleasures of the French table, which all discerning gourmets agree are without equal anywhere in the world. Wherever you choose to eat in France, from the internationally-known hotel to the modest little bistro, it is possible to enjoy either simple or elaborate dishes together with fine wines, which may be local and almost unknown or of world-wide acclaim.

A list of special dishes for which each region of France is famous is well beyond the scope of this guide, and to name but a few would be misleading since it must leave so much unsaid. The same would be true of the many wines common to each region. There are however many standard dishes which you will meet throughout France and some of these may usefully be mentioned.

The French normally take soup before dinner rather than lunch. Hors-d'oeuvre, either hot or cold, usually precede the midday meal. To name but a few of these appetizers: Bisque de homard, soupe à l'oignon, soupe au pistou (a vegetable soup flavoured with basil and very popular in the south), and consommé. The hors-d'oeuvre usually consists of mixed vegetables with tomatoes very much in evidence, or Salade Niçoise (tomato, radish, green pepper and beans). Or you may prefer oysters – in great variety – or scallops served in the shell (coquilles St. Jacques).

All the coasts of France are rich in every kind of sea-fish, shellfish and oysters. Freshwater fish is also in abundance, particularly trout, pike, carp and eels. "Matelote d'anguilles" is one of the celebrated fish dishes, though most common to the regions of the Atlantic coast; it is a stew of small eels cooked in wine with onion, garlic and egg-yolk and simmered for a long period. There are also grilled sardines, grilled mackerel, grilled salmon, grilled tunnyfish, fried whiting, soles and trout (meunière, poached, à la crème), mullet, turbot and pike (au beurre blanc, à la crème, grilled), quenelles of salmon, and, of course, frog's legs à la poulette.

All that can be said about the main dish – the "pièce de résistance" – is that whatever your choice, wherever you are served, it is almost certain to be a credit to the culinary arts. The poultry dishes are beyond compare and the visitor will surely relish chicken with tarragon (poulet à l'estragon), cock in wine (coq au vin) or turkey with chestnuts (dinde aux marrons).

Should you be at a loss over the endless choice of cheeses you will always find some of those varieties which are deservedly world celebrated: Brie, Camembert, Cantal and Roquefort. The dessert will be a choice of fruit, an ice-cream or an incomparable soufflé, macaroons, or you may find a "tourteau fromagé", a kind of cake made with soft cheese or curds, eggs, sugar and a little flour.

Again, it is pointless to attempt any classification of the wines. The great French vineyard regions have given their names to wines that are known throughout the world. Champagne, without question, produces the most widely acclaimed wine, and the choice vintages of Alsace, Bordeaux and Burgundy, the Loire and Rhône valleys, and Provence are just as worthy. If you are uncertain as to which wine you should have with your meal, ask the waiter. In the smaller restaurant he may well suggest a humble local wine that will prove as enjoyable as the most expensive one. Don't be put off if a red wine is recommended when you imagined that white was the correct choice; the French are less fussy about such matters, perhaps because they are used to more wine than we are. Where you wine and dine will depend on the thickness of your wallet, and since the French cater so admirably for all classes the following information will prove useful.

Restaurants de Tourisme whatever their rating are under an obligation to offer a special tourist menu which includes an hors-d'oeuvre, a main dish chosen from those which figure that day on the à la carte menu, and cheese or dessert. Prices, which are also reasonable for the particular grade, vary according to the category of the restaurant. There are four such categories. 4-star, de luxe restaurant offering the very finest food: 3-star, very high grade restaurant: 2-star, medium grade restaurant: 1-star, unpretentious but good restaurant.

An outstanding feature of Restaurants de Tourisme is that they must have three different specialities of their own in popular dishes, one of which must be listed on the menu each day. They must also provide well-laid tables and full facilities. They also undertake to maintain the prices they have given for publication.

De Luxe restaurants are considered worthy of three stars for cooking though the furnishings are 'not necessarily luxurious. The Michelin Hotel and Restaurants Guide lists a number of such top-grade restaurants.

Railway station restaurants somewhat surprisingly are among the best restaurants to be found in France. They have a very high local standing and many make a speciality of some of the regional dishes. Their prices are moderate for their own particular grade.

Les Routiers restaurants provide a good and plentiful meal at a very reasonable price, but without any of the luxury trimmings. You are guaranteed a good meal where you see a long-distance lorry driver breaking his journey. A number of these restaurants have formed an association known as "Les Routiers" and although they vary widely you can enter safely where you see the sign.

Self-service restaurants will be found in Paris and some other cities and they offer a wide variety of good food at very reasonable prices.

USEFUL WORDS FOR THE RESTAURANT AND CAFE

GENERAL

bar bar *m. băhr*
bill addition *f. ăh-de-se-o*ng
bottle bouteille *f. boo-tay-e*
cup tasse *f. tahss*
drink boisson *f. bo'ăhss-o*ng
egg cup coquetier *m. kock-te-eh*
fork fourchette *f. foohr-shett*
glass verre *m. vair*
knife couteau *m. koo-toh*
menu menu *m. mer-n*E
napkin serviette *f. sair-ve-ett*
plate assiette *f. ahss-e-ett*
spoon cuillère *f. kwee-yair*
table table *f. tăh-bl*
tip pourboire *m. poohr-bo'ahr*
waiter garçon *m. găhr-so*ng
waitress serveuse *f. sair-verz*
wine list carte des vins *f. kăhrt day v*ang

FOOD

apple pomme *f. pomm*
banana banane *f. băh-năhn*
beans haricots *m. ăh-re-ko*
beef boeuf *m. berf*
biscuit biscuit *m. biss-kwee*
bread pain *m. pang*

butter beurre *m. ber*
cabbage chou *m. shoo*
cake gâteau *m. gah-toh*
carrots carotte *f. kăh-rot*
cauliflower chou-fleur *m. shoo fler*
cheese fromage *m. from-ăhsh*
chops côtelette *f. koht-lett*
cream crème *f. kraym*
egg oeuf *m. erf*
fish poisson *m. po'ăhss-ong*
fruit fruit *m. frwee*
grapes raisin *m. ray-zang*
ham jambon *m. shang-bong*
ice-cream glace *f. glăhss*
jam confitures *f. kong-fe-tEEr*
lamb agneau *m. ahn-yoh*
lemon citron *m. se-trong*
lobster homard *m. omm-ahr*
marmalade confiture d'oranges *f.*
          kong-fe-tEEr dor-ahngsh
melon melon *m. mer-long*
mushrooms champignons *m. shang-peen-yong*
mussels moules *f. mool*
mustard moutarde *f. moo-tăhrd*
oil huile *f. weel*
onions oignons *m. onn-yong*
orange orange *f. or-ahngsh*
oysters huîtres *f. wee-tr*
parsley persil *m. pair-see*
peach pêche *f. paysh*
pear poire *f. po'ăhr*

peas petits pois *m. per-te po'ah*
pepper poivre *m. po'ăh-vr*
pork porc *m. por*
potatoes pommes de terre *f. pomm der tair*
poultry volaille *f. voll-ăh'e*
rice riz *m. re*
roll petit pain *m. per-te pang*
salad salade *f. săh-lăhd*
salt sel *m. sell*
sauce sauce *f. sohss*
scampi scampi *m. skang-pe*
shrimps crevettes *f. krer-vett*
soup potage *m. pot-ăhsh*
sugar sucre *m. seekr*
toast pain grillé *m. pang gree-yeh*
tomatoes tomates *f. tomm-ăht*
vanilla vanille *f. văh-nee-ye*
veal veau *m. voh*
vegetables légumes *m. leh-ghEEM*
vinegar vinaigre *m. ve-nay-gr*

DRINKS

aperitif apéritif *m. ăh-peh-re-tiff*
beer bière *f. be-air*
brandy cognac *m. kon-yăhck*
chocolate chocolat *m. shock-oll-ăh*
coffee café *m. kăh-feh*
gin gin *m. sheen*
ice glaçon *m. glahss-ong*

*lemonade citronade *f. se-troh-năhd*
liqueur liqueur *f. lee-ker*
milk lait *m. lay*
mineral water eau minérale *f. oh me-neh-răhl*
*orangeade orangeade *f. or-ahng-shăhd*
port porto *m. por-toh*
rum rhum *m. romm*
soda water soda *m. so-dăh*
tea thé *m. teh*
water eau *f. oh*
whisky whisky *m. weess-ke*
wine vin *m. vang*
    (dry, sweet, white, red, rosé) sec, doux, blanc, rouge,
    rosé *sayk, doo, blahng, roosh, roh-zeh*

* You will probably get a fizzy drink unless you specify
otherwise (". . . non gazeuse", *nong găh-zerz*). If you
want fresh orange or lemon juice, ask for:
        une orange pressée or un citron pressé
        EEn *or-ahngsh* (ung *se-trong*) *press-eh*

USEFUL PHRASES FOR THE RESTAURANT

May I (we) have a table?   Pourrais-je (pourrions-nous)
                    avoir une table?
   poo-raysh (*poo-re-*ong *noo z'*) *ăh-vo'ăhr* EEn *tăh-bl*
May we have a snack?   Pourrions-nous avoir un
                   snack?
   *poo-re-*ong *noo z'ăh-vo'ăhr* ung *snăhck*

E   65

We are in a hurry Nous sommes pressés
    noo somm press-eh

May I have the menu? Puis-je avoir le menu?
    pweesh ăh-vo'ăhr ler mer-nE

Have you any English dishes? Avez-vous des plats anglais?
    ăh-veh voo day plăh ahng-glay

I do not like highly Je n'aime pas la nourriture
seasoned food trop assaisonnée
    sher naym păh lăh noo-re-tEEr tro p'ahss-ay-zonn-eh

I like it well done Je l'aime bien cuit
    sher laym be-ang kwee

Medium-, under-done A point, saignant
    ăh po-ang, sayn-yahng

May I have some bread? Je voudrais du pain, s'il
    vous plaît
    sher voo-dray dE pang sill voo play

I will have the set lunch Je prendrai le déjeuner
(dinner) (dîner) à prix fixe
    sher prahng-dray ler deh-sher-neh (de-neh) ăh pre feeks

A little more Encore un peu
    ahng-kor ung per

That is enough C'est assez
    say ăhss-eh

May I have the wine list? Pourrais-je avoir la carte
    des vins?
    poo-raysh ăh-vo'ăhr lăh kăhrt day vang

May I have a ($\frac{1}{2}$) flask of local red (white) wine?	Pourrais-je avoir une (demie) carafe de vin rouge (blanc)?
poo-raysh ăh-vo'ăhr EEn *(der-me) kăh-răhf der vang roosh (blang)*	
I like a dry (sweet) wine	J'aime un vin sec (doux)
shaym ung vang sayk (doo)	
May I have some water?	Pourrais-je avoir de l'eau?
poo-raysh ăh-vo'ăhr der loh	
May I have some coffee?	Pourrais-je avoir du café?
poo-raysh ăh-vo'ăhr dE *kăh-feh*	
I do not like fat	Je n'aime pas le gras
sher naym păh ler grah	
What do you recommend?	Que conseillez-vous?
ker kong-say'e-eh voo	
Would you bring me an ash-tray?	Voulez-vous m'apporter un cendrier?
voo-leh voo măh-por-teh ung sahng-dre-eh	
I will come back	Je reviendrai
sher rer-ve-ang-dray	
May I reserve a table for . . . ?	J'aimerais réserver une table pour . . . ?
shaym-ray reh-zair-veh EEn *tăh-bl poohr . . .*	
May I have the bill?	L'addition s'il vous plaît
lăh-de-se-ong sill voo play	
The meal was excellent	Le repas était excellent
ler rer-pah ay-tay eck-say-lahng	

Shopping

Most shops are open from 9 a.m. to 6.30 p.m. every day except Sundays and Mondays, whilst the department stores are closed on Sundays and Monday mornings. Many food shops open up for a short time on Sunday mornings. Some chemists remain open all day Sunday and those which are closed display a list of the nearest ones to be found open.

Every province has its own specialities for the discerning souvenir hunter, all high quality products in extremely good taste as distinct from so much of the rubbish which finds its way home from the continental tour. The names themselves are a world-wide guarantee of quality. Limoges and porcelain; Brittany and lace; Quimper and pottery; colourful fabrics from the Basque country; beautiful ceramics from Vallauris. And to remind the inner man, and woman, of the palatable pleasures of the country: brandies from Charente; Kirsch from Alsace; confectionery from Auvergne; foie gras from Périgord; and of course Champagne.

The Côte d'Azur is a shopper's paradise. Apart from the fashionable boutiques, which are found everywhere and rival those of Paris, especially recommended buys are: perfumes from Grasse; lavender essence and bags; Provençal cretonnes made up into skirts, handbags and tray-cloths; olive wood ware; dolls in Niçoise costume; sweets imitating olives, mimosa etc.; glass-ware from Biot.

USEFUL WORDS AND PHRASES

(Many foodstuffs are shown in the FOOD AND WINE section.)

GENERAL

ball point stylo à bille *m.* *stee-loh ăh bee-ye*
belt ceinture *f.* *sang-tEEr*
blouse chemisier *m.* *sher-me-ze-eh*
book livre *m.* *lee-vr*
bracelet bracelet *m.* *brăhss-lay*
braces bretelles *brer-tell*
brassiere soutien-gorge *m. m.* *soo-te-ang-gorsh*
brooch broche *f.* *brosh*
buttons boutons *boo-tong*
cap casquette *f.* *kăhss-kett*
cigars cigares *m.* *se-găhr*
cigarettes cigarettes *f.* *se-găh-rett*
coat manteau *m.* *măhng-toh*
dictionary dictionnaire *m.* *dicks-e-onn-air*
doll poupée *f.* *poo-peh*
dress robe *f.* *rob*
ear rings boucles d'oreilles *f.* *boo-kl doh-ray'e*
elastic élastique *m.* *eh-lăhss-tick*
envelope enveloppe *f.* *ahngv-lop*
gloves gants *m.* *ghahng*
gramophone record disque *m.* *disk*
guide book guide *m.* *gheed*
handbag sac à main *m.* *săhck ăh mang*
handkerchiefs mouchoirs *m.* *moo-sho'ăhr*
hat chapeau *m.* *shăh-poh*

69

ink encre *f. ah*ng-*kr*
jacket veste *f. vaysst*
jumper pull-over *m.* PEE*l-oh-ve*r
lace dentelle *f. dah*ng-*tell*
lighter briquet *m. bre-kay*
lighter flint pierre à briquet *f. pe-ay*r *ăh bre-kay*
lighter fuel essence à briquet *f. eh-sah*ngss *ăh bre-kay*
lighter gas recharge *f. re*r-*shăhr*s*h*
map carte *f. kăhrt*
matches allumettes *f. ăh-*lE-*mett*
necklace collier *m. koll-e-eh*
needle aiguille *f. ay-gwee-ye*r
newspaper journal *m. shoohr-năhl*
nightdress chemise de nuit *f. she*r-*mee*z de*r nwee*
nylons nylons *m. ne-long*
pants caleçon *m. kăhl-song*
pen stylo *m. stee-loh*
pencil crayon *m. kray-yo*ng
petticoat jupon *m. s*hE-*po*ng
pipe pipe *f. peep*
pin épingle *f. eh-p*ang-*gl*
purse porte-monnaie *m. po*r-te*r-monn-ay*
pyjamas pyjama *m. pe-s*hăh-*măh*
ring bague *f. băhg*
sandals sandales *f. sa*hng-*dăhl*
scarf foulard *m. fool-lăh*r
scissors ciseaux *m. se-zoh*
shawl châle *m. shahl*
shirt chemise *f. she*r-*mee*z
shoes chaussures *f. shohss-*EEr
shoe polish cirage *m. se-răhs*h

shoe laces lacets *m. lăh-say*
silk soie *f. so'ăh*
skirt jupe *f. sh*EEP
slip combinaison *f. ko*ng-*be-nay-zo*ng
slippers chaussons *m. shohss-o*ng
soap savon *m. săh-vo*ng
socks chaussettes *f. shohss-ett*
spectacles lunettes *f. l*E-*nayt*
stockings bas *m. băh*
strap courroie *f. koo-ro'ăh*
string ficelle *f. fe-sell*
suit (man's) costume *m. koss-t*EE*m*
   (woman's) tailleur *m. tah'e-yer*
suitcase valise *f. văh-leez*
thread fil *m. feel*
tie cravate *f. krăh văht*
tobacco-pouch blague à tabac *f. blăhg ăh tăh-băh*
toy jouet *m. shoo-ay*
trousers pantalons *m. pah*ng-*tăh-lo*ng
umbrella parapluie *m. păh-răh-plwee*
undies dessous *m. der-soo*
wallet portefeuille *m. por-ter-fer'e*
watch montre *f. mong-tr*
wool laine *f. layn*
writing paper papier à lettres *m. păh-pe-eh ăh let-tr*

I want to buy ...   J'aimerais acheter ...
        shaym-ray ăhsh-teh

Will you show me some ...   Voulez-vous me montrer ...
   *voo-lay-voo me*r *mong-treh*

Have you anything cheaper   Avez-vous quelque chose de
(dearer)?   moins (de plus) cher?
  *ăh-veh voo kell-ke*r *shohz de*r *mwang (de*r *pl*E*) shair*

Have you anything bigger   Avez-vous quelque chose de
(smaller)?   plus grand (petit)?
  *ăh-veh voo kell-ke*r *shohz de*r *pl*E *grah*ng *(pe*r*-te)*

Do you have it in other   L'avez-vous dans d'autres
colours?   couleurs?
  *lăh-veh voo dah*ng *doh-t*r *koo-le*r

Can you match this colour?   Pouvez-vous l'assortir a
    cette couleur?
  *poo-vay voo lăhss-or-teer ăh sett koo-le*r

Will you deliver it (them)?   Pouvez-vous me le/la (les)
    faire livrer?
  *poo-vay voo me*r *le*r*/lăh (lay) fai*r *lee-vre*h

I will collect it later   Je viendrai le chercher tout-
    à-l'heure
  *she*r *ve-a*ng*-dray le*r*-shair sheh too-t'ăh-le*r

That's what I want   Voilà ce que je veux
  *vo'ăh-lăh se*r *ke*r *she*r *ve*r

It is not suitable   Cela ne va pas
  *se*r*-lăh ne*r *văh păh*

Could you put it (them) in   Pourriez-vous me le/la (les)
a box for me?   mettre dans une boîte?
*poo-re-yeh voo me*r *le*r*/lăh (lay) met-t*r *dah*ng *z*EE*n bo'ăht*

May I have a receipt? Je voudrais un reçu
sher voo-dray ung rer-se

Can you let me have it by ... ? Pourrais-je l'avoir pour ...?
poo-raysh läh-vo'äh poohr ...

May I try it (them)? Pourrais-je l'essayer (les essayer)?
poo-raysh leh-say-yeh (lay z'eh-say-yeh)

Can you repair this? Pouvez-vous me faire réparer ceci?
poo-vay voo mer fair reh-päh-reh ser-se

Can you have it invisibly mended? Pourriez-vous me le faire stopper?
poo-re-yeh voo mer ler fair stop-eh

How long will it take? Combien de temps cela prendra-t-il?
kang-be-ang der tahng ser-lah prahng-dräh till

THE CHEMIST **Pharmacie** (*fähr-mäh-see*)

aspirin aspirine *f. ähss-pe-reen*
bath salts sels de bain *m. sell der bang*
cotton wool coton hydrophile *m. kot-ong e-droh-feel*
cough mixture sirop pour la toux *m. se-ro poohr läh too*
gargle gargarisme *m. gähr-gäh-rissm*
laxative purgatif *m. pEEr-gäh-tiff*
lipstick rouge à lèvres *m. roosh äh lay-vr*
medicine médicament *m. meh-de-käh-mahng*

73

---

nail file lime *f.* *leem*
ointment pommade *f.* *pomm-ăhd*
plaster tricostéril *m.* *tre-koss-teh-reel*
powder (face) poudre *f.* *poo-dr*
razor blades lames de rasoir *f.* *lăhm* de*r* *răh-zo'ăhr*
sanitary towels serviettes hygiéniques *f.*
              sair-ve-ett e-she-ain-neek
scissors ciseaux *m.* *se-zoh*
soap savon *m.* *săh-vong*
sun glasses lunettes de soleil *f.* *l*E*-nayt* de*r* *soll-ay'e*
sun-tan lotion lotion pour brunir *f.*
             *loh-se-ong poohr br*E*-neer*
talcum powder talc *m.* *tăhlck*
throat pastilles pastilles pour la gorge *f.*
             păhss-tee-ye poohr lăh gorsh
toilet paper papier hygiénique *m.*
             păh-pe-eh e-she-ain-neek
tooth brush brosse à dents *f.* *bross ăh dah*ng
tooth paste pâte dentrifrice *f.* *paht dah*ng*-te-friss*

Can you make up this prescription?	Pourriez-vous me faire pré-parer cette ordonnance?
poo-re-yeh voo me*r* *fair preh-păh-reh sett or-donn-ah*ng*ss*	

Could you let me have something for . . . ?	Pourriez-vous me donner quelque chose pour . . .?
poo-re-yeh voo me*r* *donn-eh kell-ker shohz poohr*	

Upset stomach. Headache. Indigestion. Toothache. Diarrhoea.	Un estomac dérangé. Un mal de tête. Une indigestion. Un mal de dent. La diarrhée.

ung ess-tomm-ăh deh-rahng-sheh. ung măhl der tayt. EEn ang-de-shayss-te-ong. ung măhl der dahng. lăh de-ăh-reh.

I have been sunburnt	J'ai un coup de soleil

shay ung koo der soll-ay'e

My feet are blistered	J'ai des ampoules aux pieds

shay day ahng-pool oh pe-eh

I want something for insect bites	J'aimerais quelque chose pour des piqûres d'insectes

shaym-ray kell-ker shohz poohr day pe-KEEr dang-say-kt

I think it is poisoned	Je crois que c'est envenimé

sher kro'ăh ker say ahngv-ne-meh

I have a head cold	J'ai un rhume de cerveau

shay ung rEEm der sair-voh

My throat is very sore	J'ai très mal à la gorge

shay tray măhl ăh lăh gorsh

HAIRDRESSERS   **Coiffeurs** (*ko'ăhf-er*)

appointment rendez-vous *m. rahng-deh-voo*
bleach décoloration *f. deh-koll-oh-răh-se-ong*
brush brosse à cheveux *f. bross ăh sher-ver*
colour rinse rinçage *m. rang-săhsh*
comb peigne *m. payn-yer*

75

cut coupe *f. koop*
manicure manucure *f. măh-nE-kEEr*
perm permanente *f. pair-măh-nahngt*
set mise en plis *f. meez ahng plee*
shampoo shampooing *m. shahng-po'ang*
tint teinture *f. tang-tEEr*

May I make an appointment?	J'aimerais prendre un rendezvous
	shaym-ray prahngdr ung rahng-deh-voo
I want a shave	J'aimerais me faire raser
	shaym-ray mer fair rah-zeh
I want a haircut	J'aimerais une coupe
	shaym-ray EEn koop
Not too short	Pas trop court
	păh tro koohr
I would like it short	Je les veux courts
	sher lay ver koohr
I want a shampoo and set	J'aimerais un shampooing et une mise en plis
	shaym-ray ung shahng-po'ang eh EEn meez ahng plee
It is too hot (cold)	C'est trop chaud (froid)
	say tro shoh (fro'ăh)
It is not dry	Ce n'est pas sec
	ser neh păh sayk

That is excellent   C'est parfait
say pähr-fay

Photographe (*fot-og-rähf*)

black and white film pellicule noire et blanche *f.*
*payl-le-*KEEL *no'ähr eh blah*ng*sh*

camera caméra *f.* appareil photographique *m.*
käh-may-räh, äh-päh-ray'e fot-og-räh-fick

colour film pellicule en couleurs *f.*
*payl-le-*KEEL *ah*ng *koo-ler*

develop développer *deh-ver-lop-eh*

enlarge aggrandir *äh-grah*ng*-deer*

enlargement aggrandissement *m.* *äh-grah*ng*-diss-mah*ng

exposure-meter posemètre *m.* *pohz-met-tr*

filter filtre *m.* *feel-tr*

glossy brillant *bree-yah*ng

lens objectif *m.* *ob-sheck-tiff*

lens-hood parasoleil *m.* *päh-räh-soll-ay'e*

matt mat *mäht*

negative négatif *m.* *neh-ghäh-tiff*

print épreuve *f.* *eh-prerv*

range-finder télémètre *m.* *teh-leh-met-tr*

shutter obturateur *m.* *ob-*tE*-räh-ter*

tripod pied *m.* *pe-eh*

view-finder viseur *m.* *ve-ser*

Will you develop (and print) this film?	Voulez-vous me développer (et tirer les epreuves de) ce film?

voo-leh voo mer deh-ver-lop-eh (eh te-reh lay z'eh-prerv der) ser film

I would like some enlargements	J'aimerais quelques aggrandissements

shaym-ray kell-ker ăh-grahng-diss-mahng

There is something wrong with my camera	Mon appareil à photos ne marche pas bien

mong ăh-păh-ray'e ah fot-oh ner măhrsh păh be-ang

The film won't turn	Le film ne tourne pas

ler film ner toohrn păh

OTHER SHOPS

baker boulangerie *f. boo-lahngsh-ree*
butcher boucherie *f. boosh-ree*
cake shop pâtisserie *f. păh-tiss-ree*
cleaner teinturier *m. tang-rEE-re-eh*
confectioner confiserie *f. kong-feez-ree*
dairy laiterie *f. layt-ree*
draper mercerie *f. mair-ser-ree*
fishmonger marchand de poisson
    măhr-shahng der po'ăhss-ong
fruiterer marchand de fruits *măhr-shahng der frwee*
grocer épicerie *f. eh-peess-ree*
ironmonger quincaillerie *m. kang-kah'e-ree*
jeweller bijouterie *m. be-shoot-ree*

newsagent marchand de journaux *m.*
    *măhr-shah*ng *der shoohr-noh*
perfumery parfumerie *f. păhr-fɛm-ree*
shoe repairer cordonnier *m. kor-donn-e-eh*
shoe shop magasin de chaussures *m.*
    *măh-găh-*zang *der shohss-ɛɛr*
stationer papeterie *f. păh-peh-tree*

Sport, The Beach

Wherever you may be in France there is no shortage
of facilities for the sportsman, even though your interests
may be only those of a spectator – by inclination or because you do not have the necessary kit with you. Since
equipment like golf clubs and tennis rackets can be hired
in most places, the unprepared need not despair.

Most sports are found somewhere in France; soccer,
rugby (both League and Union), golf, tennis, fencing,
swimming, hunting, shooting and fishing, and even cricket.
For the motor-racing enthusiast there are internationally
famous events like the Le Mans 24 Hour race and the
Monaco Grand Prix. Cycling is very popular and the
"Tour de France" is the highlight of the year. If you are a
keen canoeist, climber or winter sportsman you will
doubtless be on holiday specifically to enjoy one or other
of these activities; France has plenty of opportunities for
each. Of course, if you suddenly feel like ski-ing (even as a

novice) you may hire skis. At Chamonix even the non-skier or climber will want to ride on the highest téléférique in the world to the top of the Aiguille du Midi, at 12,467 feet about 3,000 feet below the summit of Mont Blanc, and across the upper snow fields of the Vallée Blanche to the Italian frontier (11,370 feet).

For the majority of visitors, however, the beach will be the venue of their most strenuous activities. Along the whole length of France's 2,000 mile coastline there are more than 350 golden beaches that provide everything that you associate with a holiday by the sea.

USEFUL WORDS AND PHRASES

bathe se baigner *ser bain-yeh*
bathing cabin cabine de bains *f. kăh-been der ba*ng
bathing cap bonnet de bain *m. bonn-ay der ba*ng
bathing costume maillot de bain *m. mah'e-yo der ba*ng
bay baie *f. bay*
beach plage *f. plăhsh*
boat bateau *m. băh-toh*
bouy bouée *f. boo-eh*
canoe périssoire *f. peh-re-so'ăhr*
cliff falaise *f. făh-layz*
coast côte *f. koht*
current courant *m. koo-rah*ng
deck chair chaise longue *f. shayz long-gh*
diving board plongeoir *m. plong-sho'ăhr*
fish (n.) poisson *m. po'ăhss-ong*

fish (v.) pêcher *pay-sheh*
flippers palmes *m. păhlm*
jelly-fish méduse *f. meh-*DEEZ
pebbles galets *m. găh-lay*
raft radeau *m. răh-doh*
rocks rochers *m. rosh-eh*
sand sable *m. săh-bl*
sandhills dunes *f. d*EEN
shell coquillages *m. kock-ee-yahsh*
snorkel tuyau *m. twee-yoh*
sunshade parasol *m. păh-răh-soll*
tide marée *f. măh-reh*
water skis skis nautiques *m. skee noh-tick*
wave vague *f. văhg*

Which is the way to the beach?	Où est la plage, s'il vous plaît?
	oo ay lăh plăhsh, sill voo play
Can I hire a deck-chair (sun-shade, cabin)?	J'aimerais louer une chaise longue (un parasol, une cabine)
	shaym-ray loo-eh EEn *shayz long-gh (ung păh-răh-soll,* EEn *kăh-been)*
Can I hire some flippers?	Est-ce que je peux louer des palmes?
	ayss-ker sher per loo-eh day păhlm
Can I hire a snorkel?	J'aimerais louer un tuyau
	shaym-ray loo-eh ung twee-yoh

Where is it safe to bathe? Où peut-on se baigner sans
danger?
oo per-t'ong ser bain-yeh sahng dahng-sheh

Can I go fishing? Est-ce que je peux pêcher?
ayss-ker sher per pay-sheh

I am not a good swimmer Je ne nage pas bien
sher ner nähsh päh be-ang

Bathing prohibited "Bains interdits" *or*
"Défense de se baigner"
bang ang-tair-de, deh-fahngss der ser bain-yeh

Can I hire a sailing boat Pourrais-je avoir un voilier
(rowing, motor boat)? (un bateau à rames, à
moteur)?
poo-raysh äh-vo'äh ung vo'äh-le-eh
(ung bäh-toh ah rahm, ah mot-er)

Where can I go water- Où peut-on faire du ski
skiing? nautique?
oo per-t'ong fair dE skee noh-tick

I only want to sunbathe Je ne veux prendre que des
bains de soleil
sher ner ver prahngdr ker day bang der soll-ay'e

Is it dangerous? Est-ce que c'est dangereux?
ayss ker say dahng-sher-rer

Are there any rocks there? Y a-t-il des rochers?
e äh-till day rosh-eh

Does it shelve quickly?   Est-ce que l'on perd pied
                               rapidement?
*ayss ke*r *long pair pe-eh răh-peed-mah*ng

Is there a shower?   Y a-t-il une douche?
e ăh-t-ill EEn *doosh*

Post Office, Telephones

Post Offices in Paris are open from Monday to
Friday between 8 a.m. and 7 p.m., and on Saturdays
between 8 a.m. and noon. Main Offices are open on
Sundays and public holidays, but only for telegrams and
telephoning. Outside Paris, offices are open from 8 a.m.
until noon and from 2 p.m. to 6 p.m. Letter boxes are
painted yellow in most places but there are still a few blue
ones around. Apart from at Post Offices they are to be
found wherever there is a tobacconist displaying an
illuminated red cigar-shaped sign. Stamps may be bought
from cafés that also sell cigarettes, as well as from the
Post Office.

There are three types of public telephones in France:

1. Telephone kiosks on streets. These are square
   stainless steel kiosks with glass panels on all four
   sides. They work with coins (two 20-centime
   pieces). If the subscriber does not reply or fails to
   state the number the coins are retrieved by putting
   the receiver back. Public telephones at Le Bourget
   and Orly airports work on the same principle.

2. Public boxes in Post Offices and in the Métro work on the same principle but with a "jeton" in place of coins. Jetons are obtainable for 60 centimes at the counter in Post Offices or at the ticket office in the Métro.

3. Telephone boxes in cafés. These are the most numerous. They work on the same principle with a jeton costing 70 centimes. Only local calls can be made.

All telephone numbers in the Paris area are now made up of seven figures. In Paris itself and some suburbs the first three figures still correspond to the letters of the old exchanges.

To telephone the United Kingdom:

From a Post Office: Ask the telephone attendant at the desk. She will obtain the number and direct you to the right box.

From a private line on the automatic system: Dial 19, wait for the musical call, then dial 44 followed by the area code and the number you want. An important point to remember is that you must **not** dial the 0 which prefixes all area code numbers in the United Kingdom.

USEFUL WORDS AND PHRASES

cablegram télégramme international *m.*
        teh-leh-grähm ang-*tair-näh-se-onn-ăhl*
call appel *m.* *ăh-pell*
collection levée *f. ler-veh*

directory annuaire *m. ăhn-nE-air*
international money order mandat international *m.*
*mah*ng-*dăh* a*ng-tair-năh-se-ann-*
ăhl
letter lettre *f. lay-tr*
letter box boîte à lettres *s. bo'ăht ah lay-tr*
number numéro *m. nE-meh-ro*
post card carte postale *f. kăhrt poss-tăhl*
post office bureau de poste *m. bE-roh der post*
postal order mandat *m. mah*ng-*dăh*
register recommander *rer-komm-ah*ng-*deh*
stamp timbre *m. tang-br*
telegram télégramme *m. teh-leh-grăhm*
telephone téléphone *m. teh-leh-fon*
to telephone téléphoner *teh-leh-fon-eh*
telephone box cabine téléphonique *f.*
kăh-been teh-leh-fon-eek

**Where is the nearest post
office?**
Est-ce qu'il y a un bureau de
poste près d'ici?
*ayss-kill e ăh u*ng *bE-roh der post pray de-se*

**I want to send this post card
(letter, parcel)**
Je veux envoyer cette carte
(cette lettre, ce paquet)
*sher ver ah*ng-*vo'ăh-yeh sett kăhrt (sett lay-tr, ser păh-kay)*

I want to register this letter
Je veux recommander cette
lettre
*sher ver rer-komm-ah*ng-*deh sett lay-tr*

Are there any letters for me?   Est-ce qu'il y a du courrier
                                     pour moi?
   ayss kill e ăh dE koo-re-eh poohr mwăh

Is there a parcel for me?   Est-ce qu'il y a un paquet
                                pour moi?
   ayss kill e ăh ung păh-kay poohr mw'ăh

Here is my passport   Voici mon passeport
   vo'ăh-se mong păhss-por

May I have a telephone   J'aimerais un jeton s'il vous
counter?   plaît.
   shaym-ray ung sher-tong sill voo play

Medical Services

Under the EEC Social Security regulations visitors from the UK qualify for treatment on the same basis as the French themselves. You must complete the form CM1 (at your own Social Security office or labour exchange) no earlier than six months before travelling. You then get a certificate (E111) for use if you need treatment, plus an explanatory leaflet.

If you are suddenly taken ill and need medicine, a Chemist's is called a "Pharmacie". At night and on Sundays the Commissariat de Police will tell you where the nearest Pharmacie is that is still open. If you have a prescription from your doctor at home, it will have to be rewritten by a French doctor. Some chemists specialize in English medicines and if you have not brought (or if they

do not stock) the remedy you require they can always
recommend a substitute.

There is a British hospital on the outskirts of Paris,
the Hertford British Hospital, at 48 rue Villiers, Levallois
Perret, Seine (telephone 737–52–58 or 737–94–10).

USEFUL WORDS AND PHRASES

accident accident *m. ahck-se-dan*ng
ambulance ambulance *f. ah*ng-bE-lang*ss*
appendicitis appendicite *f. ăh-p*ang*-de-sit*
bandage pansement *m. pah*ngss-mah*ng*
bite morsure *f. mor-*sEEr
blister ampoule *f. ah*ng-*pool*
burn brûlure *f. br*E-*lEEr*
chill coup de froid *m. koo de*r *fro'ăh*
constipation constipation *f. k*ong*s-te-*pặh*-se-o*ng
cough toux *f. too*
to cough tousser *tooss-eh*
cramp crampe *f. krah*ng*p*
cut coupure *f. koo-*pEEr
dentist dentiste *m. dah*ng*-tist*
diarrhoea diarrhée *f. de-ăh-reh*
doctor docteur *m. dock-ter*
faint s'évanouir *seh-văh-noo-eer*
fever fièvre *f. fe-ay-vr*
fracture fracture *f. frăhck-tEEr*
hospital hôpital *m. op-e-tăhl*
indigestion indigestion *f. a*ng*-de-shayss-te-o*ng

influenza grippe *f.* *grip*
injection piqûre *f.* *pe-kEEr*
insomnia insomnie *f.* *ang-somm-nee*
nurse infirmière *f.* *ang-feer-me-air*
pain douleur *f.* *doo-ler*
poison poison *m.* *po'äh-zong*
policeman agent de police *m.* *äh-shahng der poll-iss*
sling écharpe *f.* *eh-shährp*
splint éclisse *f.* *eh-kliss*
sprain entorse *f.* *ahng-tors*
sting piqûre *f.* *pe-kEEr*
stomach ache mal au ventre *mähl oh vahng-tr*
sunstroke insolation *f.* *ang-soll-äh-se-ong*
surgery chirurgie *f.* *she-rEEr-shee*
temperature température *f.* *tahng-peh-räh-tEEr*
throat gorge *f.* *gorsh*
toothache mal de dent *mähl der dahng*
vomit vomir *vomm-eer*

Call an ambulance quickly Appelez vite une ambulance
ähp-leh veet EEn ahng-bE-lahngss

Call a policeman quickly Appelez vite un agent
ähp-leh veet ung ah-shang

Stand back Reculez s'il vous plaît
rer-kE-leh sill voo play

Give him (her) air	Donnez-lui de l'air
	donn-eh lwe der lair
Do not move him (her)	Ne le (la) bougez pas
	ner ler (lăh) boo-sheh păh
Is there a doctor near here?	Y a-t-il un docteur près d'ici?
	e ăh till ung dock-ter pray de-se
Have you a bandage?	Avez-vous un pansement?
	ăh-veh voo ung pahngss-mahng
I have a pain here	J'ai mal ici
	sheh măhl e-se
Bring some hot (cold) water	Apportez de l'eau chaude (froide)
	ăh-por-teh der loh shohd (fro'ărd)
Bring me a blanket	Apportez-moi une couverture
	ăh-por-teh mwăh een loo vair-teer
I am feeling very ill	Je me sens très malade
	sher mer sahng tray măh-lahd
Please bring a doctor	Appelez un docteur s'il vous plaît
	ăhp-leh ung dock-ter sill voo play
Do you have any pain here?	Avez-vous mal ici?
	ăh-veh voo măhl e-se
Where is the nearest dentist?	Où y a-t-il un dentiste?
	oo e ah till ung dahng-tisst
Will you given me an injection?	Voulez-vous me donner une piqûre?
	voo-leh voo mer donn-eh een pe-keer

Useful Information

Currency, Banks

French regulations permit the import of French bank notes up to any amount, but they prohibit the export of French notes in excess of 500 francs. Banks are open from 9 a.m. to midday and from 2 to 5 p.m. on weekdays, and are generally closed on Saturdays in the main centres. Elsewhere they are closed on Mondays and open on Saturdays. In Paris all banks open during the lunch hour, and most large banks keep a "bureau de change" open on Saturday during the summer.

A permanent exchange office is open every day at the Invalides Air Terminal from 6 a.m. to midnight, another at St. Lazare railway station from 6 a.m. to 10 p.m., another at Le Bourget airport from 8 a.m. to 10 p.m. That at Orly airport never closes. Other exchange facilities are available at main line railway stations, travel agencies and major hotels during hours when the banks are not open. You are asked to insert below the prevailing rate of exchange as this is subject to fluctuation.

10 centimes =		5 francs =
50 centimes =		10 francs =
1 franc =		50 francs =
	100 francs =	

Tipping

Where service is not included in the bill in cafés and restaurants, tips should be of the order of 12 to 15 per cent. When service is included, the very small change is usually left on the table. At hotels in which the service charge is included, it is usual to give an additional tip to hall porters and others who render additional services. Usherettes at theatres and cinemas are usually tipped around F 0·50 for showing theatregoers to their seats. Taxi drivers expect 10 to 15 per cent of the fare as tip. Guides who take parties to monuments are usually tipped between F 0·50 and 1·00.

Public Holidays to remember are: New Year's Day; Easter Monday; May 1st; Ascension Day; Whit Monday; July 14th (Bastille Day – national holiday), August 15th; November 1st and 11th; Christmas Day.

Welcome and Information Offices

These are situated in various tourist centres and operate a telex network which enables visitors to reserve hotel rooms at once. There is no charge for this special service, and you may make reservations in any of the towns that have a Welcome Office ("Accueil de France") or in their surrounding districts. Reservations in the centre itself can be made only for the same day, but in other centres in the network you can book for the following day as well. For more distant dates, reservations are best made direct with the hotels or through travel agents. Welcome Information Offices also provide a free information service and money exchange facilities.

Electric current

Although 110–115 volt 50 cycle A.C. is still the form of current most usually to be found in French hotels and houses, there is an increasing use of 220–230 volt 50 cycle A.C. and care should always be taken to check beforehand.

Public Conveniences

In hotels, restaurants, cafes and stations, look for the legend "Toilettes" or "Lavabos"; these are the most generally used signs. "Hommes" means "Gentlemen" and "Dames" (needless to say) means "Ladies". In private houses the lavatory is often called "le water" (ler vah-tair). If necessary, you may use the facilities provided by any cafe; simply ask politely and leave a small tip.

Where is the lavatory, please?	Où sont les toilettes, s'il vous plaît ?

*oo so*ng *lay to'ăh-lett, sill voo play*

British and Continental Clothing Sizes

Dresses and suits (Women)

British	34	36	38	40	42	44
Continental	40	42	44	46	48	50

Junior Miss

British	32	33	35	36	38	39
Continental	38	40	42	44	46	48

Men's suits

British	36	38	40	42	44	46
Continental	46	48	50	52	54	56

Shirts and collars

British	14	$14\frac{1}{2}$	15	$15\frac{1}{2}$	16	$16\frac{1}{2}$	17
Continental	36	37	38	39	41	42	43

Shoes

British	3	4	5	6	7	8	9	10	11	12
Continental	36	37	38	39	41	42	43	44	46	47

Hats

British	$6\frac{1}{2}$	$6\frac{5}{8}$	$6\frac{3}{4}$	$6\frac{7}{8}$	7	$7\frac{1}{8}$	$7\frac{1}{4}$	$7\frac{3}{8}$	$7\frac{1}{2}$
Continental	53	54	55	56	57	58	59	60	61

Stockings

British	8	$8\frac{1}{2}$	9	$9\frac{1}{2}$	10	$10\frac{1}{2}$
Continental	0	1	2	3	4	5

Socks

British	9½	10	10½	11	11½
Continental	38–39	39–40	40–41	41–42	42–43

Gloves are the same size as in Britain.

Conversion Tables

DISTANCES

Distances are marked in kilometres. To convert kilometres to miles, divide the km. by 8 and multiply by 5. Convert miles to km. by dividing the miles by 5 and multiplying by 8. A mile is 1 km. 610 m.

km.	miles or km.	miles	km.	miles or km.	miles
1·6	1	0·6	16·1	10	6·2
3·2	2	1·2	32·2	20	12·4
4·8	3	1·9	48·3	30	18·6
6·4	4	2·5	64·4	40	24·9
8·1	5	3·1	80·5	50	31·1
9·7	6	3·7	160·9	100	62·1
11·3	7	4·4	321·9	200	124·2
12·9	8	5·0	804·7	500	310·7
14·5	9	5·6	1609·4	1000	621·4

Other units of length

1 centimetre	= 0·39 in.	1 inch	= 25·4 millimetres
1 metre	= 39·37 in.	1 foot	= 0·30 metre (30 cm.)
10 metres	= 32·81 ft.	1 yard	= 0·91 metre

WEIGHTS

The unit you will come into most contact with is the kilogram, or kilo. To convert kg. to lbs., multiply by 2 and add $\frac{1}{10}$ of the result. One kilo (1000 gr.) is 2 lb. 3 oz.; one stone is 6·35 kg.; one cwt. is 51 kg.

grams	ounces	ounces	grams
50	1·75	1	28·0
100	3·50	2	57·1
250	8·80	4	114·3
500	17·6	8	228·6

kg.	lbs. *or* kg.	lbs.	kg.	lbs. *or* kg.	lbs.
0·5	1	2·2	3·6	8	17·6
0·9	2	4·4	4·1	9	19·8
1·4	3	6·6	4·5	10	22·1
1·8	4	8·8	9·1	20	44·1
2·3	5	11·0	11·3	25	55·1
2·7	6	13·2	22·7	50	110·2
3·2	7	15·4	45·4	100	220·5

LIQUIDS

Petrol being sold in litres, the following table (in Imperial gallons) will aid your calculations – remember that while an Imperial gallon is roughly 4½ litres, an American gallon is only 3·8 litres. One litre is about 1¾ pints, a pint is 0·57 litre.

litres	gals. *or* l.	gals.	litres	gals. *or* l.	gals.
4·6	1	0·2	36·4	8	1·8
9·1	2	0·4	40·9	9	2·0
13·6	3	0·7	45·5	10	2·2
18·2	4	0·9	90·9	20	4·4
22·7	5	1·1	136·4	30	6·6
27·3	6	1·3	181·8	40	8·8
31·8	7	1·5	227·3	50	11·0

TYRE PRESSURES

lbs. per sq. inch	17	18	19	20
kg. per sq. cm.	1k 200	1k 250	1k 350	1k 400

lbs. per sq. inch	21	22	23	24
kg. per sq. cm.	1k 475	1k 500	1k 600	1k 700

lbs. per sq. inch	25	26	27	28
kg. per sq. cm.	1k 750	1k 850	1k 900	1k 950